The
Great
Commandment
Leader

The
Great
Commandment
Leader

Becoming a Leader People Want to Follow

PAUL DORDAL

FOREWORD AND STUDY QUESTIONS BY
FERNANDO ARZOLA, JR., PH.D.

WinePressPublishing
Great Books, Defined.

WinePress Publishing (PO Box 428, Enumclaw, WA 98022) functions only as book publisher. As such, the ultimate design, content, editorial accuracy, and views expressed or implied in this work are those of the author.

ISBN 13: 978-1-4141-1918-2
ISBN 10: 1-4141-1918-6
Library of Congress Catalog Card Number: 2010912660

Contents

Section Three: Missio Dei

Acknowledgments

I COULDN'T HAVE completed this work without the support of my beautiful wife, Martha, who has loved me and journeyed beside me in my pursuit of God for more than ten years. I wish to express my deepest love and gratitude to my children—Micah, Andrew, and Naomi—who patiently endured their Poppy's absence during my times away with the army. And thank you to all my family and friends who supported and loved me through my dark days as well as my days in the light of Christ.

I'm indebted to Dr. Fernando Arzola for his assistance with the manuscript and for his friendship and partnership while we ministered together in the Bronx. Also, special thanks go to Claudia Schwartz for her keen insights into the original manuscript.

I would also like to thank the members of First Alliance Church (NYC) and Crestmont Alliance Church for allowing me to learn how to be a leader in their churches. For my mentors and colleagues: Rev. Richard Borg, Dr. John Ellenberger, Rev. Fr. David Flores, Rev. Arthur Gaunt, Rev. Ed Glover, Rev. Jim Jensen, CH (COL) Kenneth Kirk, Rev. Richard Liptak,

Rt. Rev. Alex McCullough, Dr. Mickey Noel, Dr. Jeff Norris, Rev. Angel Ortiz, Dr. Michael Scales, Rev. John Soper, Rev. Joe Toomey, and especially Dr. David Schroeder and the members of our Starbucks Prayer Group.

Thank you as well to the more than 1,250 soldiers of the 336th Military Police Battalion (Forward), whom it was my privilege to serve as chaplain "downrange" during Operation Iraqi Freedom (2009–2010).

Foreword

THE MARKETPLACE IS flooded with materials on leadership. From the practical to the philosophical, leaders are taught ways of thinking and behaving to become more effective. Paul Dordal's *The Great Commandment Leader* reminds us that the primary aim and end of Christian leadership is to love. While this may seem obvious, leadership as a ministry of love is often overlooked, minimized, and even dismissed.

Dordal begins with the concept of *imago Dei*. This is appropriate and immediately challenges those of us in leadership to question if we reflect the image of God. Do others see the image of God in our leadership?

> We were made in the image and likeness of God (Genesis 1:26) according to human nature. In other words, humanity by nature is an icon or image of deity: The divine image is in all humanity. Through sin, however, this image and likeness of God was marred and we fell. When the Son of God assumed our humanity...the process of our being renewed in God's image and likeness was begun. Thus, those who are

joined to Christ through faith...begin a process of re-creation, being renewed in God's image and likeness.[1]

This book helps us to begin the discovery and recovery process of Christian leadership. Dordal argues "the transformation process is accomplished by teaching others to be obedient to God, primarily through the proclamation of the gospel, personal example, spiritual formation, and godly service so God can transform those they lead back into the loving image of God. The end goal of Great Commandment leaders is to help people be transformed into the image of Jesus Christ."

For Dordal, the transformation process into becoming a Great Commandment leader is rooted in the heart of the law: to love God and to love man. Authentic Christian leadership demands both the worship of God and service to others. Venerable Bede states, "Neither of these two kinds of love is expressed with full maturity without the other, because God cannot be loved apart from our neighbor, nor our neighbor apart from God."[2]

While it is apt to traditionally refer to this pericope as the Great Commandment, it is more adequate to understand it as the greatest commandment. That is, not only is it significant, but it is, as Jesus states, "first" and "second" of all the commandments. About this commandment, Origen explains that Jesus's "statement contains something necessary for us to know, since it is the greatest. The others—even to the least of them—are inferior to it."[3] Therefore, the Great Commandment leader paradigm is viewed through the lens of the love of God and the love of others as the greatest of all leadership functions.

There is much to learn from this book. As a Christian educator, I am particularly pleased by the myriad of models presented, especially in Section Three. These not only serve as helpful teaching guides but also underscore the diverse ways of incarnating Great Commandment leadership. Yet to read *The Great Commandment Leader* as merely an alternative leadership template misses the point. It is a call to focus on what is eternally significant in Christian leadership: worship, service, and love.

—**Fernando Arzola Jr.,** PhD
August 2010
New York City

SECTION ONE

Imago Dei

Prelude: The Aisle of a Thousand Chairs

JOSH TANNER SQUIRMED on a rusting, metal folding chair alongside five hundred of his fellow soon-to-be college graduates. Little kids in their Sunday best played tag between the rows, and proud parents beamed as they clicked pictures of their sons and daughters.

It was a chilly, drizzly late May afternoon in Dunn's Bridge, Indiana. But Josh didn't notice the weather because he was daydreaming about his future. He relished this day and remembered what his professors had told the students at the graduation breakfast. "This is *your* day! Enjoy it!"

Josh noticed the official photographer on stage and wondered if he should do something crazy before shaking the president's hand at his small, liberal arts college. Should he do a cartwheel, give a thumbs-up to the crowd, or shout something silly?

No, this is my college graduation day, he thought. *I ought to be dignified.*

Josh looked around at the other graduates. What was next for his friends and classmates? An advanced degree? A good-paying job? A promotion? Who was going to become famous or powerful?

Maybe it'll be me.

Once his degree was in hand, nothing could stop him from realizing his dreams. At the baccalaureate the night before, he'd heard an encouraging speech about how important a good education was to succeed in life. The speaker had waxed eloquently and quoted Francis Bacon, who said, "Knowledge is power." And Josh certainly felt powerful today.

He smiled. One of the graduates had drawn a Superman S on top of his mortarboard; another had glued a Superman figurine to the top of his.

The ceremony was filled with pomp and circumstance—and they played the Elgar song, too. The school's professors were dressed in all their regalia and attired with velvet stripes on heavy, black robes. The smiling academics proceeded down the aisle of a thousand chairs, their hoods purple, red, blue, and green. What did the colors mean? Who cared! The display looked great, and it was all for Josh and his fellow graduates.

The college's chairman of the board spoke briefly. He told the assembled graduates and their families that the board members were unpaid volunteers. He went on to say that graduation day was like their pay day. The fruit of all their volunteer labor was to see the graduates go on to their successful futures.

Josh was excited about beginning his new career as a sales manager at a large New York City-based retail electronics firm. He was graduating *summa cum laude* with a degree in organizational leadership and felt like he was well prepared to succeed as a leader. In fact, he believed leadership was in his blood. His father was a successful businessman himself, and he'd helped Josh get the job in New York.

The next speaker was an older man, a well-known pastor from Ohio.[4] Josh dreaded sitting through another hour-long motivational speech. Last year when Josh had ushered at graduation, the keynote speaker had gone on and on, and no one could remember what he'd said ten minutes afterward.

The pastor stepped to the podium and surveyed the crowed, not saying anything for an uncomfortably long moment. *Maybe he forgot his speech*, Josh thought.

Just then the speaker opened with an intriguing question. "Why are you here?" He paused again for effect, scanning the crowd with caring eyes, and repeated the question. "Why are you here?"

Josh sighed in annoyance. *To graduate, you knucklehead!*

"Do you really know why you're here, the reason for your existence?" the pastor asked. "Let's do a little call and response. When I ask, 'Why are you here?' you're all going to reply with four little words. I'm going to do this about twenty times over the next half hour. Are you tracking with me?"

Several of the graduates yelled out "amen" and laughed.

Oh, good. He's only going to talk for half an hour. We can get out of here and get to the real reason why we're here: to celebrate our great accomplishment and get on with life.

The keynote speaker continued, "I bet you think that you've learned a lot in college. But with these four words, I'm going to teach you in a few minutes more than you've learned in the last four years. I want you to remember these four little words because you're on this planet for this reason and this reason alone. If you don't get it today, I fear you may never get it."

Though mildly interested in what the old man had to say, Josh was more focused on all the cool things people had written on their mortarboards. *Why didn't I think of something witty to write on* my *hat?*

"Here they are, the four little words that will change your life. Why are you here? To love God back!"

He shouted, "Why are you here?"

Most of the five hundred graduates yelled in unison, "To love God back!"

"Why are you here?"

"To love God back!"

"Why are you here?"

"To love God back!"

The rest of the famous pastor's speech focused on God's love for humanity and our responsive love for Him.

Josh found the exchange and the speech amusing but didn't really understand what any of it had to do with graduation. All he could think about was being in New York City in a few short weeks to begin his great, new career.

Unfortunately, Josh's first foray into the world of leadership was a disaster. He couldn't figure out how to manage some of the lower-performing salesmen and thought the sales force didn't respect him because he was young. But the reality was that Josh spent a lot of time trying to convince them that he knew what he was doing when in reality he didn't. Always trying to impress his followers, Josh wasn't interested in learning the ropes. Instead, he talked endlessly about the leadership principles and theories he'd learned in college.

Just a few months after starting his dream job, senior management at the electronics firm let him go due to incompetence. Josh's supervisor said he needed more experience and training. Confused and devastated, Josh returned to his studio apartment on the Upper East Side and wondered what went wrong.

Introduction

JOSH TANNER'S STORY isn't unique. Though he'd received a good education and maybe even learned from an excellent leadership example or two in his life, he had yet to learn how to become the kind of leader people wanted to follow.

American society has an overabundance of leadership training programs and degrees offered in our colleges and universities. Unfortunately, many of these programs aren't designed to actually develop good leaders. Instead, most academic leadership programs emphasize theoretical models and teach practical ways to exercise management principles.

I don't want to sound too negative about leadership education. Training of this kind is important and useful to those called to be leaders, but before you can practice good leadership, you must first learn what it means to be a good leader! This will require docking the "leader ship."

DOCKING THE "LEADER SHIP"

The idea of docking the "leader ship" came to mind after I read R. Scott Rodin's book *Stewards in the Kingdom*. Rodin suggests that one problem in the teaching of biblical stewardship in churches and seminaries is that teachers often forget to help students first appropriate what being a steward means. The critically omitted prerequisite questions are "What are the character qualities of a good steward" and "What is the truth about possessions that I must understand prior to practicing good stewardship?" Rodin suggests that we dock the "steward-ship" until we understand what it means to become effective stewards.

Sadly, a similar problem emerges from leadership studies and literature. An overemphasis on methodology encourages students to do what leaders do before they've learned what being a good leader means. We haven't sufficiently asked and answered the most important question. What is a godly leader, and how do I become one before I begin learning and practicing leadership principles and techniques? Bypassing this important question is why so many well-educated people fail in leadership. They try to put into practice what they've yet to become. They've emphasized *doing* leadership rather than *being* good leaders. The proverbial cart has been placed before the horse.

DEFINING A LEADER

We now understand that a critical difference exists between being a good leader and practicing leadership. Therefore, defining who a good leader is before teaching what he or she does helps us to right the ship before we leave the port.

Any ethically derived definition of a leader must start with the leader's character. The US Army has a field manual on leadership that boils the leadership process down to "BE-KNOW-DO."

The army correctly starts the leadership conversation by focusing on the character of the leader—"BE." A leader, the army says, is someone who has exceptional character and lives life by an ethical set of values. The apostle Paul also articulates that a godly leader is someone who has character that is above reproach (1 Tim. 3:2). Each potential leader must wrestle with his or her preparedness to lead based on whether the person's character has been developed to the extent that followers will trust the person. Prior to evaluating intellect or ability to achieve results, the leader is first and foremost a certain type of person—someone with a distinct quality. Therefore, he is before he does.

Second, a leader is someone who has an optimistic vision. That is, he or she seeks to improve the future of the individuals, groups/organizations, and/or the wider community he or she leads. Though followers and leaders may have similar character qualities, what distinguishes leaders from followers is their capacity to articulate and achieve a compelling vision.

To that end I offer a working definition: an effective leader is someone of impeccable character and dynamic vision whom others want to follow because they've developed trust in the leader to do the right thing for them, their organization/group, and the wider community.

DEFINING LEADERSHIP

Most leadership definitions I've encountered center on the concept of influence. Leadership theorists and scholars usually define leadership as the activity of influencing individuals or groups to achieve some mutually understood goal, even if it isn't something followers are particularly interested in achieving themselves.

Well-known leadership author John Maxwell reduces leadership to three words—"Leadership is influence, nothing more, nothing less." The obvious question we must ask in light of Maxwell's definition, however, is "Influence to what end?" What should be the outcome of that influence?

The outcome of any truly ethical leadership must be the positive transformation of the individual followers, the organization or group, and the wider community. Therefore, any definition of leadership as influence should focus primarily on the process of creating positive, catalytic change (transformation) for individuals, groups/organizations, and whole communities.

THE GREAT COMMANDMENT

So what does all this have to do with the Great Commandment in the Bible?

You may have lately noticed a lot of books about Jesus and leadership. Some titles available today include *The Leadership Lessons of Jesus*, *Jesus on Leadership*, *The Leadership Secrets of Jesus*, *Jesus: CEO*, and *The Leadership Genius of Jesus*. This book, however, doesn't necessarily focus solely on the person of Jesus as a leader, though He certainly is the best leader anyone could emulate. Instead, we're going to focus on what Jesus said was the most compelling command in the Bible and how it interacts with becoming and being a good leader. This book is based on the biblical imperative Jesus revealed to be the most important one in life: love.

> "One of them, an expert in the law, tested him with this question: 'Teacher, which is the greatest commandment in the Law?' Jesus replied: "'Love the Lord your God with all your heart and with all your soul and with all your mind.' This is the first and greatest commandment. And the second is like it: 'Love your neighbor as yourself.'"
>
> —Matt. 22:35–39

When potential leaders truly grasp what Jesus says in the Great Commandment, they will unearth a brand new paradigm of being a leader. They will also discover a new motivation to achieve greater things for the common good. Leadership priorities and practices will take on a new emphasis, with positive personal, organizational, and whole community transformation as the end state. It truly is a *great* commandment.

Now, before you assume that love cannot be an acceptable basis for leadership, let me emphasize that we are not talking about romantic (Greek: *eros*) love or even brotherly (Greek: *philadelphia*) love. This love, as we'll understand, isn't simply the emotional feeling of love; it's what the Greek Bible calls "agape." The agape form of love is a spiritually understood love. It's a love that sacrifices, serves, and puts the interests of others before your own. The apostle Paul defined agape love in 1 Corinthians. "Love is patient; love is kind. It does not envy, it does not boast, it is not proud. It is not rude, it is not self-seeking, it is not easily angered; it keeps no record of wrongs. Love does not delight in evil but rejoices with the truth. It always protects, always trusts, always hopes, always perseveres" (13:4–7). Love is an action word, not one that only describes an emotion. This is the same love God provides for His people.

OVERVIEW OF THE BOOK

In three sections this book describes (1) the kind of character and motivation the Great Commandment leader possesses, (2) how such a leader can naturally develop trust among those he or she leads, and (3) how transformation (lasting positive change) can occur as a result of practicing six powerful leadership paradigms.

To fully comprehend the Great Commandment leader model, we first must understand two key concepts, which form the basis of our entire discussion.

First, the Great Commandment leader recognizes and understands that God deeply loves and cares for him or her.

The Greek philosopher Socrates said that the most important pursuit in life is to know oneself. What Socrates missed, however, is the understanding that self-knowledge is important only in regard to a deep knowledge of our Creator God and a correct understanding of His love for us. This is what *loving self* means in the Great Commandment—to have received and appropriated the amazing, outrageous, wonderful love of God. Without that appropriation, our ability to love God back and both love and care for others is severely diminished (1 John 4:19).

Second, by receiving God's love in Christ, Great Commandment leaders possess the ability to truly love God and others. They will "know and rely on the love God has for [them]" (1 John 4:16), which will give them the power to love God and their neighbors. The love of Jesus will motivate them to love and lead just as Jesus did (2 Cor. 5:14).

I will further discuss these key concepts in the next three chapters of Section One. In Section Two we will focus on the concept of incarnational presence as a prerequisite of building trust with our followers. Once we've given most of our attention to what being a Great Commandment leader means, in Section Three we will develop six transformational paradigms for the practice of Great Commandment leadership.

This radical new approach to becoming a leader will challenge you at various levels of your spiritual development. Please take time at the end of each chapter to review and answer the application questions before moving on to the next chapter. You will also gain greater understanding of this book's truths and principles if you read and study it with a friend, colleague, or small group.

Chapter Review Questions

1. What is the difference between being a leader and practicing leadership?

2. How does one become a good leader?
3. What is the ultimate goal of leadership?
4. The measure of the Great Commandment leader's effectiveness is sacrificial love. How does this fact inform your understanding of leadership?
5. What are the two key concepts of a Great Commandment leader?

Chapter 1

Receive God's Love

Appropriating God's Love for You

THE GREAT COMMANDMENT may seem like a straightforward message. Love God with everything you've got, and love others with the same passion. But when the Great Commandment says we should love our neighbors as we love ourselves, what exactly does the term "love ourselves" mean?

For many, the ancient Greek myth of Narcissus might be an applicable metaphor for how they understand self-love. In the myth the Greek gods bestowed upon Narcissus the most handsome appearance in the world. To retain his beauty, his only requirement was never to look at his own reflection. If he did so, the penalty would be death.

One day while Narcissus hunted in the woods, the nymph Echo saw Narcissus and fell in love with him. She couldn't communicate her love for him because she could only repeat what she'd heard others say; hence the name Echo. In his vanity Narcissus wanted nothing to do with Echo. Unable to speak her own words, she pined for his affection. In fact, she pined so long and hard that she withered away. All that remained was the echo of her voice.

The gods were displeased with Narcissus because he'd rejected Echo, so they led him to a shimmering lake. There, for the first time, Narcissus saw his own reflection and couldn't move from staring at his beauty. Trapped, he neither ate nor drank and eventually faded away. A daffodil (genus: narcissus) sprouted in his place.

Many may be unfamiliar with the myth of Narcissus or the flower by the same name, but most are aware of the personality disorder called "narcissism." Definitions of *narcissism* include "someone in unhealthy love with himself," "self-love that shuts out everyone else," and "having an exceptional interest in yourself." Unfortunately, everyone is afflicted by this disorder to some degree. In our sinful condition we're more concerned about ourselves than about others (Ezek. 34:1–3).

In her book *Generation Me,* author Jean Twenge laments that the "Millennial Generation," the group born between 1978 and 1994, has adopted a philosophy of extreme individualism and personal needs fulfillment that supersedes all other concerns. This problem, Twenge states, has its roots in the institutionalization of the self-esteem movement of the 1970s. I would add to her thesis that a "me culture" has infected almost all Western society, a problem that will continue long into the future.

For most of the "me culture," the only way to be happy is to have others meet all their emotional, physical, and material needs. Those who continue to believe their needs haven't been met focus on themselves even more—to the exclusion of others. They feel utterly empty and see themselves as victims. They often reach out for help and needs fulfillment from all the wrong sources. Like Narcissus, those in the "me culture" are trapped and focus only on themselves. Without God's love in their hearts, we see the metaphor of Narcissus being applied even further, for they experience spiritual death.

When the Great Commandment speaks of self-love, it doesn't refer to a narcissistic focus on oneself or some form of human self-fulfillment. Instead, we should understand loving ourselves in humility and selflessness. The apostle Paul said, "Do not think of yourself more highly than you ought, but rather think of yourself with sober judgment" (Rom. 12:3). To correctly love self simply means we should care for others just as much as we naturally care for ourselves and our own needs. Philippians 2:4 says, "Each of you should look not only to your own interests, but also to the interests of others." The apostle Paul repeats this theme when he says that "husbands ought to love their wives as their own bodies. He who loves his wife loves himself" (Eph. 5:28).

GOD MEETS OUR EVERY NEED

I believe, however, that having our own needs met as leaders enables us to meet the needs of others and love our neighbors as ourselves. Yet, Great Commandment leaders believe wholeheartedly that the one true God will meet their needs completely. God provides not only for the leader's sake but so the leader might become a conduit of God's love to others.

God is the Creator of all, the Sustainer of all, and the Source of all good things. "Every good and perfect gift is from above, coming down from the Father of the heavenly lights, who does not change like shifting shadows" (James 1:17). Jesus told us how much God loves us. "Why do you worry, saying, 'What will I eat?' or 'What will I drink?' or 'What will I wear?' For nonbelievers worry about all these things, but your heavenly Father knows that you need them. So put God first, seek His Kingdom and His righteousness, and He will provide all these things for you" (Matt. 6:31–33, author's paraphrase).

Great Commandment leaders depend on God to meet all their needs because they believe God, as their leader and provider, is trustworthy. God is the only true and satisfying source of needs fulfillment. The apostle Paul said, "God will meet all your needs according to his glorious riches in Christ Jesus" (Phil. 4:19). Every leader needs to unreservedly believe and appropriate this remarkable truth.

THE CHARACTER OF GOD

The question is, do you believe God is trustworthy and able to meet your every need?

We've already stated that an effective leader has impeccable character. When you think about God, our ultimate leader, what mental picture comes to your mind? What is God's character like? Jesus told many stories about God so His followers would know Him more intimately. He most often spoke about His gracious Father in heaven, who abundantly loves and cares for His children.

Yet many see God as a gruff old man obsessed with oppressive rules and regulations; He judges people based on whether their good deeds outweigh their bad. To many, God is out of touch or out to get them if they mess up. Unfortunately, many often obtain this portrayal of God from ill-informed family and friends, the media, and, sad to say, even some churches. Worse, a poor image of God might be due to an abusive or absent earthly father.

Another picture of God is the more accurate, biblical one. God is spirit and perfect love; He feels sympathy for us and is patient with our wrong understanding of Him. Throughout Scripture we read about this God of love. "For the Lord is good and his love endures forever; his faithfulness continues through all generations" (Ps. 100:5). Scripture describes God more as good and loving than any other way. That's why the apostle John explained the essence of God by simply saying, "God is love" (1 John 4:8). The character of the all-powerful, all-knowing, ever-present, perfect God of the universe is marked by an outrageous love for the crown of His creation, you and me. Hence, we should understand that God's basic character quality is perfect love.

Maybe you disagree with the image of a loving heavenly Father because you read in the Bible about a jealous God, who sometimes gets angry and pours out His wrath on unrepentant sinners. But you need to understand that God in His perfection experiences righteous indignation and corrects injustice when He deems it necessary. Yet that quality of his character doesn't negate His love and eternal goodness. In fact, it proves it all the more.

The point many need to clearly understand is that it is because of God's amazing love for us that He needs to right wrongs. King Solomon said, "My son, do not despise the Lord's discipline and do not resent his rebuke, because the Lord disciplines those he loves, as a father the son he delights in" (Prov. 3:11–12). It is out of His love that all His other character traits flow. I like the way Henry Blackaby put it: "God would cease to be God if He expressed Himself in any other way than perfect love!"[5]

The correct image of a loving Father is the one we must appropriate to effectively lead others. Jesus embodies this loving image, and Genesis reminds us that God originally created us in this image (Gen. 1:27). Therefore, the Great Commandment leader personifies the *imago Dei*, the image of a loving God through Christ.

RECEIVING THE FATHER'S LOVE

Throughout Scripture God is portrayed as the God who loves us. Imagine that: the almighty Creator of the universe loves you and cares about you personally with an endless source of love. God gives us His love as a gift, which comes in the form of His only Son, Jesus Christ, who died for our sins. But like a Christmas gift opened but neglected, we often unwrap God's love but never experience it. For whatever reason—whether unforgiveness, pride, bitterness, or guilt—many refuse to unwrap and receive the gift of God's love for them. By refusing God's gift of love, many continue to search in vain for a way to fulfill their spiritual and emotional needs.

God wants to bridge the divide that exists between Him and His creation. He wants to pour out His amazing gift of love on each of His children. Yet our sin, arrogance, and selfishness keep us from enjoying the wonderful relationship God wants to have with us. To love ourselves correctly, then, we need to accept God's gift of love. But how do we receive it?

To receive God's love, we need only to put our faith and trust in His Son, Jesus Christ, and what He did for us on the cross. This is the good news, the gospel of salvation in Christ. Jesus said if we want to be obedient to God, we will "believe in the one he has sent" (John 6:29). The apostle Paul said if we turn from our sinfulness, if we believe Jesus is God and rose from the dead, we will be saved (Rom. 10:9). The apostle Peter proclaimed, "Repent and be baptized, every one of you, in the name of Jesus Christ for the forgiveness of your sins. And you will receive the gift of the Holy Spirit" (Acts 2:38). To enjoy His eternal gift of love, we simply must be willing to turn our lives over to God and accept His offer of forgiveness and salvation through Jesus Christ.

Though what I'm about to say may seem simple to those who've been Christians for a while, we cannot simply rush past the amazing truth and grace of the gospel. Some readers may have never heard and understood the good news of Jesus Christ.

If you've received the gift of God's love through Jesus, you've become a child of God, and God has changed your life dramatically. "Yet to all who received [Jesus], to those who believed in his name, he gave the right to become children of God" (John 1:12). Radically freed from the burden of sin and filled with the Spirit of Christ, you can begin to love others with an unending source of love. That's why those who recognize their many sins are forgiven can love much, Jesus said, and why those who refuse His forgiveness love little (Luke 7:47). Clearly, the reception of God's love through Jesus is critical if we're going to love Him back and love our neighbors.

The apostle Paul wrote, "But God demonstrates his own love for us in this: While we were still sinners, Christ died for us" (Rom. 5:8). God communicates His love not only in words but also in concrete actions; He demonstrates His love for us. Again, love is personified action we do in service for others. That's why one of the most famous passages of Scripture reminds us that "God so loved the world [you and me] that he *gave* his one and only Son, that whoever believes in him shall not perish but have eternal life" (John 3:16, emphasis added). Jesus Christ is the source of God's amazing love for us. God sent His Son into the world to save us (John 3:17).

Furthermore, we must understand that God didn't give us this love because we've deserved it or earned it. His love is His grace to us. "This is how God showed his love among us: He sent his one and only Son into the world that we might live through him. This is love: not that we loved God, but that he loved us and sent his Son as an atoning sacrifice for our sins" (1 John 4:9–10). The apostle Paul reminds us that God's love and mercy in Christ embody the grace that led us back to God. "But because of his great love for us, God, who is rich in mercy, made us alive with Christ even when we were dead in transgressions—it is by grace you have been saved" (Eph. 2:4–5). God simply wants to pour out His amazing love on us by His grace in Jesus through the Holy Spirit (Rom. 5:5; 2 Thess. 2:16).

In the army, when a soldier dies on the battlefield, normally a memorial service soon follows. Invariably during the service, someone will quote the well-known Scripture: "Greater love has no one than this, that he lay down his life for his friends" (John 15:13). Being willing to sacrifice oneself for another is part of the core values of being a soldier, the highest service anyone could render. God Himself offered Jesus Christ for our sins so we might receive His perfect love and forgiveness.

Unfortunately, too many leaders are stunted in their ability to truly care for others and lead in love because they carry around the baggage of past failures, regrets, selfish desires, and emotional pain. Because they've not surrendered their pasts or futures to God, including unresolved guilt, unforgiveness, bitterness, and brokenness, they cannot appropriate the love and forgiveness He offers and therefore are incapable of loving God and others. But Great Commandment leaders who truly receive the total forgiveness of Christ and the love of God in full measure are able to move on and become effective conduits of God's love to others. They will possess not self-confidence but the confidence of knowing that God loves them and has called them into leadership.

CHOSEN FOR LOVING LEADERSHIP

Most leaders have a sense of being uniquely called to their positions, but they may not be able to articulate a "calling," especially if they're nonbelievers. Nevertheless, God has chosen or "called" all leaders through whatever group or organization they're a part of (Rom. 13:1).

God lovingly calls His chosen people into leadership. In fact, leadership is a unique spiritual gift God bestows to certain people (Rom. 12:8; 1 Cor. 12:28; Eph. 4:11–12, 1 Peter 4:10–11). Yet to some degree God calls every adult to lead (family, community role, religious roles), and that's why it's important to understand that God has chosen and called us all according to His love.

The apostle Paul calls us "God's chosen people, holy and dearly loved" (Col. 3:12). To another group of Christians, he reminds them that they are brothers and sisters "loved by God, that he has chosen" (1 Thess. 1:4). When you doubt your leadership ability or calling, look to the truth of God's Word and remember that God has called you in love for His purposes. When we become followers of Jesus, we enter into a wonderful spiritual family. When we lead as followers of Jesus, we do so in the wonderful love of our heavenly Father. "How great is the love the Father has lavished on us, that we should be called children of God! And that is what we are!" (1 John 3:1).

CHRIST IN YOU, THE HOPE OF GLORY

Being in God's family and His love wasn't an easy concept for me to understand when I first made the decision to become a Christ follower. For many years I relied on my own strength, education, or personality to lead.

While attending the Alliance Theological Seminary, however, one of my professors, Dr. Martin Sanders, introduced me to the truth of being "in Christ." Though I had already served in several church leadership roles, I was unsure of myself and lacked confidence in my calling. As a young Christian, I had yet to comprehend the truth of being "in Christ."

After intensely studying the apostle Paul's letter to the Ephesians, I found that the apostle articulated no less than twenty-five times that we will find our being and fullness "in Christ." My eyes were opened not only to the person of Christ but also to His love. I discovered "Christ in you, the hope of glory" (Col. 1:27). Amazingly, God didn't pour His love on you after you became a follower of Christ but before when He chose you in love. "For he chose us in him before the creation of the world to be holy and blameless in his sight. In love he predestined us" (Eph 1:4–5). Don't let that truth escape your attention. Before time began, God chose you in His love to be part of His redemptive plan.

With this new understanding I shifted my thinking away from what I thought I needed to what Christ had already accomplished for me. My thinking shifted away from what I wanted to the ultimate good God wanted for me, and away from what I thought I lacked to what His Spirit had supernaturally provided.

The fact is, we were spiritually dead before we came into a relationship with Christ. "But because of his great love for us, God, who is rich in mercy, made us alive with Christ" (Eph. 2:4–5). Again, it is out of God's amazing love for us that we find our being and purpose.

Now listen to the apostle Paul as he prays that we might more deeply understand the love God has for us who are in Christ.

"I pray that out of His glorious riches he may strengthen you with power through his Spirit in your inner being, so that Christ may dwell in your hearts through faith. And I pray that you, being rooted and established in *love*, may have power, together with all the saints, to grasp how wide and long and high and deep is the *love* of Christ, and to know this *love* that surpasses knowledge—that you may be filled to the measure of all the fullness of God."

—Eph 3:16–19, emphasis added

The apostle Paul reminds us that being in Christ is where we find the love of God and are enabled to love God and others. Great Commandment leaders then are impersonators of God. They don't merely mimic His love but allow Christ's love to shine through them. We are called to be "imitators of God, therefore, as dearly loved children [to] live a life of love, just as Christ loved us and gave himself up for us as a fragrant offering and sacrifice to God" (Eph. 5:1–2).

In addition, this truth of being in Christ and Christ being in us is found throughout the New Testament, not just in the letter to the Ephesians. Romans 8 reminds us that as we are in Christ we're no longer under condemnation for our past sins (v. 1). Ephesians 2 tells us that God has ordained work for us to accomplish (v. 10). Romans, Galatians, and Ephesians tell us that God has received us into a new and wonderful spiritual family (Rom. 12:5; Gal. 3:26–28; Eph. 3:6). Ephesians 2 says that God has given us heavenly authority and power (vv. 6–7). And the list goes on.

The table below describes the many wonderful ways Jesus meets our needs as we live in Him and He in us.

Table 1: How Christ Fulfills Our Needs Through
His Loving Care

What Christ Gives Us	Verses	What Christ Gives Us	Verses
Fresh Start/ New Life	2 Cor. 5:17	True Freedom	Gal. 2:4; 5:1
God's Favor and Grace	1 Tim. 1:14; 2 Tim. 1:9	Purpose and Meaning	Phil. 3:13–14; Col. 1:28
Vitality for Living	1 Cor. 15:22	Holiness and Righteousness	Eph. 4:24
A Deep Sense of Joy	1 Thess. 5:16–18	Freedom from Condemnation	Rom. 8:1
Hope for the Future	2 Tim. 2:10; 1 Thess. 4:16	A Deep Relationship with God	Eph. 2:13
Ultimate Success	2 Cor. 2:14	Blessings from God	Eph. 1:3

When Great Commandment leaders appropriate Christ in them, they become not self-confident but Christ-confident to lead like Jesus leads. Their needs are met through their intimate relationship with God through Christ.

ABIDING IN THE LOVE OF CHRIST

Though we possess the confidence of Christ, we leaders will still face many difficulties. "In this world you will have trouble. But take heart! I have overcome the world" (John 16:33). All leaders face adversaries, even if they are righteous and good. They constantly encounter challenges and an ever-changing operating environment. When those challenges and difficulties mount, leaders get stressed. How leaders handle stress indicates their character. Blowing your stack, retaliating against those who oppose you, and allowing anger to get the best of you can jeopardize your reputation with those whom you lead.

In his letter to his protégé, the apostle Paul told a young bishop, "The Lord's servant must not quarrel; instead, he must be kind to everyone, able to teach, not resentful. Those who oppose him he must gently instruct, in the hope that God will grant them repentance leading them to a knowledge of the truth, and that they will come to their senses and escape from the trap of the devil, who has taken them captive to do his will" (2 Tim. 2:24–26).

Once a woman at our church was angry with our youth pastor and elders. I invited her to express her grievances to our elders, but suddenly she directed her anger toward me. I was about to let her have it when one of my elders tapped my leg as a reminder to keep my anger in check. Unfortunately, a caring friend hasn't always been nearby to restrain me. Each time I lose my temper with others, those I lead trust me a little less. Thankfully, as I've grown older and abided more in the love of Christ, my ability to restrain my anger has grown.

How do leaders refrain from "losing it" on occasion and harm the trust factor with those they lead? The answer again comes from the love of God. Great Commandment leaders will firmly fix their eyes on Jesus and abide in His love. To abide in Jesus means to rest or even hide in the love of God. Just as Jesus said, "As the Father has loved me, so have I loved you. Now remain in my love" (John 15:9).

Remaining in the love of Jesus also speaks to persevering in the faith. So many Christians, however, receive God's love and grace with great fanfare and excitement only to peter out over time (Matt. 13:3-9;18-23). Jude reminds us, however, to "keep yourselves in God's love as you wait for the mercy of our Lord Jesus Christ to bring you to eternal life" (Jude 1:21).

Though many leaders are known for their fierce self-reliance and independence, Great Commandment leaders are completely dependent on God for their needs. Their confidence, authority, and power come from their relationship with Christ. Most importantly, the Great Commandment leader leans on God for His sustaining care and love. "And so we know and rely on the love God has for us. God is love. Whoever lives in love lives in God, and God in him" (1 John 4:16).

We must stay deeply connected to Jesus to remain in His love. Using the imagery of a plant and its fruit, Jesus shows us that "[He is] the vine; [we] are the branches. If a man remains in me and I in him, he will bear much fruit; apart from me you can do nothing" (John 15:5). As you abide in Christ's love, you will be successful in your leadership roles. If you try to lead in your own power, however, you will not only fail but also accomplish nothing of lasting value.

Through their daily, intimate, even moment-by-moment worship of God, Great Commandment leaders constantly remember Christ's love. They are awash in His love, communing with Jesus through prayer and meditation on His reassuring Word. Abiding in Christ's love is how they are able to love God back and love those they lead.

Though they are passionate about achieving results for the kingdom, Great Commandment leaders, while abiding in Christ's love, are concerned about caring for and loving those they lead, just as God has done for them. If you find yourselves leading individuals in ministry or in the workplace, your followers should be able to say, "All my other supervisors cared about was my work, but you cared about me as a person."

As we will see more deeply in a later chapter, Great Commandment leaders are concerned not only about the success of the mission or achieving organizational goals but also with the personal, positive transformation of those they lead. They have this concern because of God's great love flowing through them by the Spirit of Christ.

Filled with God's love and abiding in Christ, Great Commandment leaders find it almost impossible not to love others. They are overcome with the graciousness, forgiveness, and mercy of God. Therefore, in utter gratitude they return to God and others the love they have received.

Chapter Review Questions

1. What lessons about leadership and humility can we learn from the story of Narcissus?
2. What connections can we make between the myth of Narcissus and the biblical story of Adam and Eve?
3. How might the evolution of narcissism cause the spiritual death of a leader?
4. How should Great Commandment leaders understand or measure their own worth?
5. How can Great Commandment leaders have their needs met?
6. How does our image of God inform our understanding of leadership?

Chapter 2

Loving God Back

WHEN YOU FINALLY "grasp how wide and long and high and deep is the love of Christ," your first reaction and hopefully ongoing response will be incredible gratitude toward God (Eph. 3:8). As the apostle Paul explains, you will "know this love that surpasses knowledge [and will be] filled to the measure of all the fullness of God" (Eph. 3:19). The love that surpasses knowledge is the appropriation of the complete forgiveness of sins offered by Jesus Christ. Once we fully realize what Jesus accomplished on the cross for us, the natural response is to joyfully praise God with all our hearts, understanding, and strength (Mark 12:33). But for some this isn't always the case.

Jesus tells the story of a servant who owed a certain king millions of dollars, an unimaginable sum of money for that time. When the servant appeared before the king to pay his debt, he begged the king for more time. Amazingly, the king extended mercy to the servant and canceled the debt. Afterward, the servant ran into a man who owed him a few dollars and immediately demanded that the man pay his debt. When the man couldn't pay, the servant had him arrested and thrown in jail.

When the king heard about this incident, he summoned the servant and said, "You wicked servant! I canceled all that debt of yours because you begged me to. Shouldn't you have had mercy on your fellow servant just as I had on you?" (Matt. 18:32–33). The king told the jailers to torture the servant until he paid his debt. Jesus then says this is how His Father in heaven will treat us if we fail to forgive those who have offended us.

Many see this story, often called the parable of the unmerciful servant, as one of justice; unforgiving people will not be forgiven. Yes, in the end God will right all the wrongs evil, unrepentant humans have committed. But we should consider another angle to this story.

Maybe the story should be called the parable of the ungrateful servant. The servant's normal response should have been to be filled with inexpressible joy and gratitude after the king forgave his overwhelming debt. You see, when we realize the amazing love and forgiveness God offers us, when we realize we're incapable of paying off the debt of our sinfulness, our ongoing response should be one of outrageous gratitude toward the One who forgave us. Apparently the servant in Jesus's story didn't fully accept the king's love and forgiveness. That's why he was incapable of showing love and forgiveness to the man who owed him so little.

Throughout Scripture Jesus tells stories of unsuspecting people receiving undeserved mercy, compassion, and forgiveness from an outrageous God who deeply loves them. Some return that love, but sadly others don't.

Great Commandment leaders are different because they have fully appropriated God's love and forgiveness, receiving healing in their souls so they can love God back in utter gratitude and thanksgiving. How do we love the God who has loved us so amazingly? We love the things He loves.

Loving the Things God Loves

I heard a story of a young professional man who hated only two things in life. First was eating out because it was too expensive. Besides, the food wasn't always better than what he could make at home, and most restaurants were too noisy. Second, he hated opera because the stories were silly and old. Even though a translation of the words was broadcast on a screen above the stage, he couldn't stand reading the supertitles.

One day the young man fell in love with a woman in his office. After getting up the nerve, he asked her out on a date. She agreed. When he picked her up at her house, he asked what she was interested in doing. She'd heard of a fantastic new Russian restaurant and wanted to try it.

"Do you like to eat out?" she asked.

"I love going out to eat!" he replied.

They had a great time and scheduled another date for the following week. When he arrived to pick her up, she said she'd acquired two tickets to *Madama Butterfly*, the famous Puccini opera.

"Do you like the opera?" she asked.

"I love going to the opera!" he replied.

At this point we might ask the young man an important question. Do you think you will build a good relationship by lying to the one you love? But the young man might say he wasn't lying. Because he loved this woman so much, his heart changed, and he began to love the things she loved. As we love God back, this is our call—to fall in love with the things God loves.

This is the concept of *The Five Love Languages*, a bestselling book on relationships. The book describes the successful relationship in which marriage partners show how much they love their partners by meeting their unique needs, by loving the things they love. The apostle Paul reminds us of this goal in his advice to men in marriage relationships: "Husbands ought to love their wives as their own bodies. He who loves his wife loves himself" (Eph. 5:28-29). This ability to radically change should come naturally when you truly love someone. If we love ourselves correctly, appropriating the love of God, we will know how to love God and others.

How do we show God we love Him? Scripture makes it clear that God most enjoys when His creation authentically worships Him (Ex. 20:2–6; Neh. 9:6). Jesus said to a confused woman, "A time is coming and has now come when the true worshipers will worship the Father in spirit and truth, for they are the kind of worshipers the Father seeks" (John 4:23).

The Great Commandment leader, filled with the Spirit of God, shows his or her love to God by worshipping Him in at least five different ways: (1) engaging in joy-filled, grateful praise; (2) being a good steward of time, talent, and treasures for God's purposes; (3) enjoying intimate communication with Him; (4) getting to know God through His Word; and (5) being obedient to His commands.

Praise

The Bible paints many different pictures of worship to God through sacrifice, dance, confession, singing, the public reading of God's Word, shouting, and even crying before the Lord. We want to show our love back to God out of our joy-filled gratitude. At sporting events, live concerts, or movies at the theater, we often scream and/or clap for our favorite players or performers. These expressions are a form of worship. We ascribe worth to sports figures and entertainers by adoring their performances. Shouldn't we at least do the same and more for Him who deserves so much more of our love and admiration?

The apostle Peter says, "Though you have not seen him, you love him; and even though you do not see him now, you believe in him and are filled with an inexpressible and glorious joy" (1 Peter 1:8). We can begin to express that "inexpressible" joy when we "sing psalms, hymns and spiritual songs with gratitude in [our] hearts to God" (Col. 3:16). To some degree God views our singing to Him as our humble service, a way to abandon ourselves to Him. This verse is especially applicable to men who may think singing publicly is unmanly.

At one church I pastored, many men didn't sing during the praise time of our worship service. Unfortunately, this problem rubbed off on the young boys. I knew that the adult example would be the primary way the children would learn how to show gratitude to God. One day I met with the young boys and told them the story of mighty King David, one of the fiercest warriors in the Bible. This is the same king who slew the giant Goliath and killed a lion and a bear with a knife when he was only a boy. After a major victory in battle, however, King David danced in the streets of Jerusalem to show utter worship of God (2 Sam. 6:14). David was responsible for the majority of the songs in the Bible. Though he was one of the fiercest warriors in the Bible, he was also a fierce worshipper. Maybe David could be known as a "Worshipping Warrior."

I asked the boys, "If the most awesome warrior in the Bible could sing and dance for the Lord, why can't we? Don't you want to be a worshipping warrior, too?" After that teaching, many boys understood that they could release their inhibitions and sing praises to God in grateful worship.

King David instructs us, "Sing praises to God, sing praises; sing praises to our King, sing praises. For God is the King of all the earth; sing to him a psalm of praise" (Ps. 47:6–7). Love of God includes our whole being—mind, body, soul, and spirit. As we offer these to the Lord, our mouths will open in praise to Him who loves us so much. Through songs of praise, we sing in response to God's love. "I will sing of the Lord's great love forever; with my mouth I will make your faithfulness known through all generations. I will declare that your love stands firm

forever, that you established your faithfulness in heaven itself"
(Ps. 89:1–2).

King David is an excellent example of the Great
Commandment leader. He loved God with all his heart, soul,
mind, and strength. Though he had serious flaws, David was a
man after God's own heart (1 Sam. 13:14).

Stewardship of God's Gifts

Another way we worship God is through joy-filled stewardship of His abundant gifts to us. God loves us so much that
He gave us the gift of eternal life through Jesus Christ; He also
gave us the gift of the Holy Spirit as a guarantee of our future
inheritance (Eph. 1:13–14). In addition, He gives us special
empowerments through spiritual gifts (see 1 Cor. 12; Rom. 12;
Eph. 4; 1 Peter 4).

As mentioned before, "every good and perfect gift is from
above, coming down from the Father of the heavenly lights"
(James 1:17). When we understand God as our almighty Creator
and loving Father, we realize we're simply the managers of God's
good gifts to us. Because God created all things, He owns all
things. God actually owns the time, talents, and treasure we
sometimes think we possess. Moses emphasized this fact when
he gave the written Word to the Israelites. "To the Lord your
God belong the heavens, even the highest heavens, the earth
and everything in it" (Deut 10:14). The psalmist proclaims that
the "earth is the Lord's, and everything in it, the world, and all
who live in it; for he founded it upon the seas and established
it upon the waters" (Ps. 24:1–2). The apostle Paul reminds us
that our freedom is also a gift from God. "You are not your own;
you were bought at a price" (1 Cor. 6:19–20). When we use
His gifts to serve others, we show God that we love Him and
therefore bring Him glory.

In one episode of *Seinfeld*, the popular show on TV, Elaine, the on again/off again girlfriend of the show's star, receives a birthday gift she doesn't like. Later, when she is invited to a friend's birthday party, she doesn't have time to buy a gift. She simply rewraps the gift she didn't like and gives it to the unsuspecting recipient. Elaine is eventually exposed and cast as a horrible person. She did the unpardonable–she regifted!

The show portrayed regifting as an act only incredibly shallow people would do. In the realm of God's gifts, however, God highly encourages us to be regifters. We should use the gifts God gives "for the common good" (1 Cor. 12:7; also see 1 Peter 4:10). Therefore, the gift of leadership God bestows isn't for you but for the benefit of others (see Rom. 12:8).

If we truly believe everything belongs to God (Col. 1:16), one of the most important ways we show God that we love Him is in how we manage the gift of money He entrusts to us as stewards. Jesus often used stories about money to show that God wants us to be good stewards of all His gifts (see Mat. 25:14–30). Jesus knew we would struggle in the area of worship through giving. That's why He said, "No servant can serve two masters. Either he will hate the one and love the other, or he will be devoted to the one and despise the other. You cannot serve both God and Money" (Luke 16:13).

Loving God back as Great Commandment leaders means we use God's gifts of time, talents, and treasures for His purposes and glory.

Prayer or Intimacy

Showing God we love Him doesn't imply that we constantly try to impress Him. When we love God, we do so by faith (Heb. 11:6). God doesn't want us to think that the only way we can please Him is by being vocal in praising Him, using His gifts to serve others, or exercising our faith in actions. God, who is omniscient and knows our innermost thoughts (Ps. 139), wants to spend quality time with us. He wants us to get to know Him through times of intimacy.

Our connection to God through our minds and souls should include time reflecting on His Word and in prayer with Him. As Great Commandment leaders abiding in the love of Christ, we should eagerly desire to spend quality time with God.

The ancient Desert Fathers and Mothers, the Church's earliest monastics, had a saying about intimacy with God that went something like this: "If I miss one day of spending time with God, I can still sense His presence with me. But If I miss two days in intimacy with Him, I begin to notice that I'm walking in my own strength. And if I go three days without spending significant time with my Lord, all the people around me begin to notice."

Any deep, loving relationship requires intimate communication. Jesus loved spending time with His Father. "Jesus often withdrew to lonely places and prayed" (Luke 5:16). The night before Jesus decided who His twelve apostles would be, "[He] went out to a mountainside to pray, and spent the night praying to God" (Luke 6:12). Without setting aside time to abide with Jesus, a lack of godly vision will severely impair our decision-making abilities.

It isn't so much that we must daily hide ourselves for many hours at a time in hermetic solitude, but, as the apostle Paul says, we should "be joyful always; pray continually; give thanks in all circumstances, for this is God's will for you in Christ Jesus" (1 Thess. 5:16–18). Praying continually means focusing our moment-by-moment thoughts on God and seeking His fellowship.

It is out of our deep gratitude to God that we want to meet with Him, knowing how much He loves and cares for us. The apostle Paul reminds us to pray with gratitude without worry. "Do not be anxious about anything, but in everything, by prayer and petition, with thanksgiving, present your requests to God" (Phil. 4:6). Though God has called all leaders to accomplish an eternally important mission, He wants us to spend quality time with Him.

This idea of intimacy with God was difficult for me to comprehend until I had my own children, who are all extremely bright and creative. They constantly want to impress me with their new abilities and knowledge. I'm proud of all my children's accomplishments, but my favorite time is simply hugging them and spending quality time with them in our family room. I know my children love me when they simply want to spend time with me. Likewise, God, our heavenly Father, knows we love Him when we spend significant time with Him, not because we have something to ask Him, but just because we want to.

Worship through His Word

Again, worship isn't limited to praise, stewardship, and prayer. We also love God back when we pursue Him by applying our minds to His Word. When I served as an assistant pastor at First Alliance Church in New York City, I was so busy on Sundays that I was unable to participate in the time of corporate worship. I was so distracted with other responsibilities that I couldn't even pay attention to God's Word delivered through the pastor's sermon.

Though I maintained a daily devotion of Scripture reading, I still yearned to hear God's Word preached, to worship through the Word in community. The answer to my dilemma was to attend another church, Times Square Church, during the week when services weren't being conducted at my church. There I received excellent exposition of the Word and was able to partake in the Lord's Supper.

At the time Times Square Church offered a wonderful music ministry and boasted a dynamic eighty-member choir. When

I sat in the balcony, I noticed that many of the worshippers enthusiastically sang and danced in their seats during the praise time. When the preacher came forward to speak, however, many of these exuberant worshippers checked out. Some even fell asleep before he preached the first word. Many loved to engage in praise through the music, loving God through their souls and emotions, but they didn't worship Him with their minds.

To truly love someone, you must get to know that person. If you're going to love God back, you will be joyfully interested in His Word. The Word of God is His special revelation, His direct communication to us. Through His Word, God speaks to us, shows us His loving character, and tells us how to live a holy life. In the Old and New Testament, we find that though the earth will someday pass away, the Word of God will last forever.

We should emulate King David, who loved God's Word and understood its power. "I will bow down toward your holy temple and will praise your name for your love and your faithfulness, for you have exalted above all things your name and your word" (Ps. 138:2).

The Word of God is the Great Commandment leader's manual for success. One of the more interesting questions many in leadership circles ask is this: "How do you define success?" For some, the question applies to ministry or business growth (in academic settings they call it "nickels and noses"); for others the question applies to personal wealth, the kind of house they live in, or the kind of car they drive. Still others cite their many friends or connections. What's eternally important, however, is not how *we* define success but how God does.

After Moses died, God spoke to Joshua, the new leader of His people, and said, "Do not let this Book of the Law depart from your mouth; meditate on it day and night, so that you may be careful to do everything written in it. Then you will be prosperous and successful" (Josh 1:8). This is success that comes when we know and obey God's Word!

Knowing and obeying the Word of God shows our love for God and deepens our understanding of His love for others. Again, don't miss this. The biblical definition of *success* is knowing God and obeying Him. "'Let him who boasts boast about this: that he understands and knows me, that I am the Lord, who exercises kindness, justice and righteousness on earth, for in these I delight,' declares the Lord" (Jer. 9:24).

Obedience

Quite a difference exists between knowing about God and being obedient to Him. The apostle John reminds us, "If anyone obeys his word, God's love is truly made complete in him" (1 John 2:5). Jesus said we should tell the whole world about Him, not just to know about Him but to obey His every command (Matt. 28:18–20).

Years ago I enjoyed a cup of coffee with a friend who was a non-practicing Jew. We often talked about faith issues, and I again told her about what I'd recently learned about Jesus. Though she wasn't offended, she wondered if I was interested in anything else, such as sports, politics, or books. I admitted that I liked those things, but I asked her, "If someone knew the truth about life and didn't share it, what would you think of that person?"

"Oh sure, and the truth will set you free!" my friend replied sarcastically.

"Did you know that it was Jesus who said that?" I asked.

She laughed, surprised. "Wow, I know something about Jesus!"

Unfortunately, both religious and nonreligious people often misquote the phrase "the truth will set you free." In the context of this statement—obedience to Christ's commands—however, we understand the freedom God's truth brings. "If you hold to my teaching, you are really my disciples. Then you will know the truth, and the truth will set you free" (John 8:31–32). This verse offers an if/then proposition. Only when you follow Jesus will you know the truth, and then that truth will set you free.

Obeying God's commands is by far the most important way to show Him gratitude and love. Jesus often repeated to the disciples that obedience to God's commandments was evidence of our love for Him. "If you love me, you will obey what I command....If anyone loves me, he will obey my teaching. My Father will love him, and we will come to him and make our home with him" (John 14:15, 23). Similarly, a child's obedience to his parents is a sign of respect and love. Obedience is how children love their parents back.

What are the commandments Jesus told us to obey? Of course, Jesus commanded us to be merciful, to be compassionate, to be forgiving, and to honor all the moral laws found in the Old Testament (Matt. 5:17–19). However, the system of moral laws in the Old Testament was extensive, so Jesus boiled His commands down to one: love each other. "If you obey my commands, you will remain in my love, just as I have obeyed my Father's commands and remain in his love....My command is this: Love each other as I have loved you" (John 15:10, 12). The apostle John repeated this concept and also clarified it. "And this is love: that we walk in obedience to his commands. As you have heard from the beginning, his command is that you walk in love" (2 John 1:6). Jesus said the whole world would know we were His disciples if we simply loved each other (John 13:35).

We now can see a cyclical action developing as we move into the next chapter. As God loves us and we receive His love, we naturally want to love Him back. God's Word tells us that one of the primary ways we can show our love for Him is to love one another. We love God supremely when we love the things He loves. And as we have learned, He loves His people supremely.

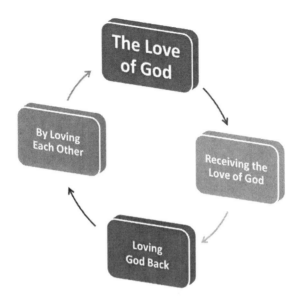

Chapter Review Questions

1. What lessons about leadership and forgiveness can we learn from the parable of the unmerciful servant?
2. How might leaders balance doing things they don't like with doing things they should do for others?
3. What are some worshipful ways Great Commandment leaders can show their love to God?
4. How should Great Commandment leaders understand their use of time, talent, and treasure?
5. How does the quote from the Desert Fathers help us more deeply examine the importance of prayer and leadership?
6. How does abiding in God help leaders more effectively abide with the people they lead?

Chapter 3

Loving God's People

IT SHOULD COME as no surprise that we should consider the love of God's people as an extension of loving God back. The abundant love God deposits in each Great Commandment leader will flow back to God and His people. To love God's people is to love God back. If you worship fervently in your church services or spend hours in meditative intimacy with God but have no love for the people around you, God considers your worship vain (Matt. 15:8–9). It doesn't matter how religious you think you are, "for in Christ Jesus belonging to a particular tradition or religion is of no value. The only thing that counts is faith expressing itself in love" (Gal. 5:6, author's paraphrase).

Therefore, you cannot say you love God without expressing a corresponding loving action toward His people. The apostle John was adamant on this point. "If anyone says, 'I love God,' yet hates his brother he is a liar. For anyone who does not love his brother, whom he has seen, cannot love God, whom he has not seen" (1 John 4:20). Earlier in the same book, the apostle says, "Let us not love with words or tongue but with actions and in truth" (1 John 3:17). James also warns us that a faith without loving action is a dead faith (James 2:26).

Again, we shouldn't worry about how we may be able to love so much. "Since God so loved us, we also ought to love one another" (1 John 4:11). This is not an exercise in manufacturing care and compassion for others; it's simply an outflow of Christ's love through His Holy Spirit living in us (Gal. 5:22). Great Commandment leaders always remember they can love because God first loved them.

RADICAL LOVE

When we talk about love as the basis of leadership, it is again not just the emotional kind of love that may first come to mind. Great Commandment love is a radical kind of love, a sacrificial, selfless, almost self-abasing kind of love. This is why Jesus surprisingly said to His disciples, "A *new* command I give you: Love one another. As I have loved you, so you must love one another. By this all men will know that you are my disciples, if you love one another" (John 13:34–35, emphasis added). Though the Old Testament often repeats this command and Jesus often repeats it in the New Testament, Jesus's emphasis on it and His standard of what it looks like are quite new. It is a radical kind of love.

We've already noted that the study of leadership can be helpful in the development of leaders. Nevertheless, we recognized that mere knowledge of leadership theories or techniques doesn't make a leader effective. The apostle Paul knew this truth almost two thousand years ago when he wrote, "Knowledge puffs up, but love builds up" (1 Cor. 8:1). That is the radical nature of Great Commandment leadership. You don't learn it, you live it.

The love we show others can be radical in at least five ways.

Love for Enemies

First, Jesus doesn't limit the kind of people to whom we should show love. In the new, radical concept of love, Great Commandment leaders understand that they can't simply love those who love and support them. They also must love their enemies.

> But I tell you who hear me: Love your enemies, do good to those who hate you, bless those who curse you, pray for those who mistreat you. If someone strikes you on one cheek, turn to him the other also. If someone takes your cloak, do not stop him from taking your tunic. Give to everyone who asks you, and if anyone takes what belongs to you, do not demand it back. Do to others as you would have them do to you. If you love those who love you, what credit is that to you? Even "sinners" love those who love them. And if you do good to those who are good to you, what credit is that to you? Even "sinners" do that.
>
> —Luke 6:27–33

Jesus gave us a great example of radical love in His encounter with the so-called rich young ruler. In this story a pious young man asked Jesus how he could be assured of eternal life. Though his religious formation seemed sincere, Jesus noticed that he was arrogant. Jesus wasn't always gentle with the arrogant religious people of His day, but in this story we see Jesus's gentle heart even toward those who opposed Him.

After the religious young man told Jesus about his pietistic perfection, "Jesus looked at him and *loved him.* 'One thing you lack,' he said, 'Go, sell everything you have and give to the poor, and you will have treasure in heaven. Then come, follow me'" (Mark 10:21, emphasis added). When I read that verse, I imagine how much God loves us, even when we're sinful and disobedient. Then He redirects us toward holiness and obedience. This is also how we can love those who dislike us—by loving them wholeheartedly and redirecting their arrogance or hatred into something positive.

Radical love was part of Jesus's continuing message to His disciples, especially to those who considered themselves to be religious or holy. People have a natural tendency to form homogeneous groups, to be cliquish. But when those groups exclude others, disunity, jealousy, and discrimination flourish. Great Commandment leaders are bridge builders to those who may be outside their group, organization, or community. They show love even to those opposed to them.

Love of Strangers (Hospitality)

Second, we express radical love through hospitality. Great Commandment leaders not only reach out in love to those who oppose them but also show hospitality to complete strangers. Jesus said He would invite into heaven those who invited strangers into their lives. "I was a stranger and you invited me in....I tell you a truth, whatever you did for one of the least of these brothers of mine, you did for me" (Matt. 25:35, 40).

In 1986, after returning from a trip to London, I was redirected to Frankfurt, Germany, instead of to Ramstein, where my car was parked. I was in the main *bahnhof* (railway station) and had no money for the train. In just a few hours, I was supposed to be in formation with my army unit in Ansbach one hundred kilometers to the south.

I was frantically looking for a soldier to take me to a local base when I spotted a uniformed young man waiting near the tracks. After I explained my situation, he reached into his pocket and without hesitation gave me the forty deutsche marks I needed for the fare. I asked for his address so I could mail him a check, but he said, "Don't worry about it. But make sure if you're ever in a similar situation and someone needs your help that you won't hesitate either."

Jesus wants us to show love to those who aren't used to it. In one of His remarkable teachings, He challenged us to show radical love. "When you give a luncheon or dinner, do not invite your friends, your brothers or relatives, or your rich neighbors; if you do, they may invite you back and so you will be repaid. But when you give a banquet, invite the poor, the crippled, the lame, the blind, and you will be blessed. Although they cannot repay you, you will be repaid at the resurrection of the righteous" (Luke 14:12–14).

As a leader you should never assume that the person you're talking to or meeting for the first time is somehow beneath you or unworthy of your attention. You never know if that person is someone God sent to be a blessing to you or someone to whom He wants you to show His love. For many in other cultures, hospitality isn't so radical, but we Westerners need to relearn how to show God's love through hospitality.

Love for Those Who Are Different

Third, Great Commandment leaders recognize, celebrate, and develop the differences of the people they lead. Jesus broke all sorts of societal taboos to show that ethnic, religious, gender, and racial prejudice were sins against the God who created all people in His loving image. In addition, the twelve disciples were about as different from each other as can be. Yet this was the leadership team Jesus put together: two spoiled teenagers, a thief, a despised tax collector, an insurrectionist, several fledgling fishermen, and an insecure naysayer. Because of God's love flowing through them, this motley crew changed the world forever.

Too often leaders surround themselves with people of similar backgrounds, skill sets, and personalities. This tendency usually results in "group think"; after a while creativity is stifled, and bad decisions go unchecked. Because God has created each person with unique talents and skills, Great Commandment leaders, bearing the *imago Dei*, love those they lead equally. They help their followers develop their God-given, unique gifts and talents, recognizing that true unity is expressed in diversity.

Love That Is Self-Sacrificing

Fourth, radical love is a self-sacrificing love. Jesus loved us so much that He sacrificed Himself for us. He took the humiliation and punishment we deserved so He could set us free from the eternal effect of sin. Remember, "God demonstrates his own love for us in this: While we were still sinners, Christ died for us" (Rom. 5:8). The apostle Paul tells husbands to love their wives with the same love Jesus showed when He laid down His life for the church (Eph. 5:2).

From John 3:16 we've already learned about the amazing love God has for us in Christ Jesus, but what about the other John 3:16? In 1 John 3:16, we learn how to love others sacrificially. "This is how we know what love is: Jesus Christ laid down his life for us. And we ought to lay down our lives for our brothers." Again, Christ's loving actions toward us show us how to love others.

Love That Is Always Forgiving

Perhaps the most important radical love lifestyle Great Commandment leaders live out is forgiveness. When the disciples asked Jesus how they should pray, He said they should ask God to "forgive us our debts, as we also have forgiven our debtors" (Matt. 6:12). Great Commandment leaders, released from the burden of their own sinfulness, recognize that God's forgiveness prompts them to forgive others. To develop a lifestyle of forgiveness, we must ask God to remove our desire for revenge (Deut. 32:35). In our service to others, our radical love "covers over a multitude of sins" (1 Peter 4:8).

God proves His love for us by forgiving all the wrongs we commit against Him and others. In the Old Testament we learn about a God who is "slow to anger, abounding in love and forgiving sin and rebellion" (Num. 14:18). The psalmist reveled in the fact that "you are forgiving and good, O Lord, abounding in love to all who call to you" (Ps. 86:5). After His resurrection, Jesus commanded the disciples to go into the whole world to be His agents of love and forgiveness. "Again Jesus said, 'Peace be with you! As the Father has sent me, I am sending you.' And with that he breathed on them and said, 'Receive the Holy Spirit. If you forgive anyone his sins, they are forgiven; if you do not forgive them, they are not forgiven'" (John 20:21–23).

The radical nature of forgiveness isn't simply the activity of pardoning in reaction to sins committed. It is a lifestyle of understanding God's absolute grace and sovereignty, of knowing that Jesus died once and for all for the forgiveness of sin (1 Peter 3:18). Therefore, we develop a heart of forgiveness, looking to show the love of God to others—no matter what they may have done to offend us.

We find one of the best modern examples of forgiveness in the tragedy in Nickel Mines, Pennsylvania. In 2006 a distraught man entered an Amish schoolhouse for girls and shot ten of the girls, killing five. Then he killed himself. Soon after the murders, the families of the victims went to the killer's wife and communicated their forgiveness of her husband. Amazingly, they also gave the wife some of the financial assistance pouring into the community.

Many people were amazed, including several journalists, who wrote articles expressing disbelief at the amazing love and forgiveness the Amish showed the murderer's family. The world's disbelief confused the Amish. From their vantage point, they had done what they always did, forgiving those who had sinned against them. Their lifestyle of forgiveness allows them to heal more quickly and love more readily.

The apostle Peter asked Jesus how many times we should forgive those who sin against us. Jesus used hyperbole to express that we should always forgive (Matt. 18:21–22). The apostle Paul urges us to "bear with each other and forgive whatever grievances you may have against one another. Forgive as the Lord forgave you. And over all these virtues put on love, which binds them all together in perfect unity" (Col. 3:13–14). God's forgiveness and love should be our greatest motivators to extend the same to others.

MOTIVATED TO LOVE

Great Commandment leaders are highly motivated because of the incredible love and forgiveness God has given to them. As such, they no longer look at their jobs as professions or careers because they see all they do as a mission or ministry to the Lord. "Whatever you do, work at it with all your heart, as working for the Lord, not for men, since you know that you will receive an inheritance from the Lord as a reward. It is the Lord Christ you are serving" (Col. 3:23–24).

Leadership studies have put forth many theories of motivation; however, none of them start with this amazing truth: "For Christ's love compels [urges] us, because we are convinced that one died for all, and therefore all died" (2 Cor. 5:14). Christian leaders don't need common external motivators such as accolades, commendations, pay raises, or benefits packages to excel. They understand their holy obligation to serve Christ and His people out of love. This is not to say that they turn down awards or raises when they are offered, but recognition and rewards do not motivate the Great Commandment leader. The love of God motivates us to love.

When I served in Iraq, I noticed two different kinds of leaders. Some leaders were convinced that their jobs were critical to the success of the mission and therefore didn't need much motivation. They understood they served a bigger purpose than themselves. Sadly, others struggled to find ways to increase their desire to work and the level of their output. When I asked several of the low performers how they felt about the mission or their jobs, they said they didn't think they made much of a difference. Though we can encourage others in various ways, it is difficult to motivate them unless they experience a change of heart.

The Great Commandment leader, who understands God's love and that he or she works for the greatest purpose, doesn't need the motivation of material or emotional rewards. Remember, God has already met our needs in Christ Jesus, so we already have all the motivation we need. "Praise be to the God and Father of our Lord Jesus Christ, who has blessed us in the heavenly realms with every spiritual blessing in Christ" (Eph. 1:3; also see Phil. 4:19).

At the end of 1 Corinthians 13, the "love chapter," the apostle Paul ends his monologue with these words: "And now these three remain: faith, hope and love. But the greatest of these is love" (v. 13). All three can be motivators, but love is the greatest because only love is eternally necessary. Faith and hope are temporally beneficial while we live here on earth, but love will last forever. In 1 Thessalonians, the apostle Paul praises church members motivated by faith, hope, and love. He says he continually remembers their "labor prompted by love" (1 Thess 1:3). God's love through Christ as a motivator for leadership is an untapped resource for many. It is the power of Christ's love that gives the Great Commandment leader his or her strength and passion to lead.

ONE ANOTHERS

Because God's love motivates and supernaturally empowers us, we are able to love others. But in what specific ways should we show love to others as we lead them? The simplest way the Great Commandment leader can learn how to share the love of God with others is to study the many "one anothers" in Scripture. At least forty-four instances of "one another" appear in the New Testament alone. Of course, Jesus told us that to "love one another" was the most important aspect of being His disciple.

God also instructs us to "greet one another" (2 Cor. 13:12), "bear with each other" (Col. 3:13), "admonish one another" (Col. 3:16), "consider others better than yourselves" (Phil. 2:3), "instruct one another" (Rom. 15:14), "pray for each other" (James 5:16), and many more. God doesn't leave us to wonder how a leader should act in regard to those he or she leads. The Bible clearly delineates the character qualities of the Great Commandment leader.

THE BENEFITS OF BEING A LOVING LEADER

As we've already seen, God intends that the love He pours into those who follow Jesus be poured back to God and His people. But like the TV sales pitch, wait, there's more! If it wasn't enough just to have God's love flowing through you, God promises great benefits to those who love Him and love their neighbors.

The apostle Paul says to the church at Rome, "And we know that in all things God works for the good of those who love him, who have been called according to his purpose" (Rom. 8:28). Here's the key: those who love God know without a shadow of a doubt that He works for the good of those in His perfect, loving will. This promise is near and dear to all who claim Christ as their Lord and Savior.

What benefits await the Great Commandment leader? "As it is written: 'No eye has seen, no ear has heard, no mind has conceived what God has prepared for those who love him'" (1 Cor. 2:9). Not only will good come about because of our love of God, but the apostle Paul says the human mind is unable to fathom the wonderful things God will do for those who live according to His will and love.

Finally, the apostle wants us to know that "the man who loves God is known by God" (1 Cor. 8:3). This awesome truth is easy to gloss over. Many like to know important people and want to be known by them. I've often heard the question, "If you could spend a few hours with any person from history, who would it be?" Some choose one of the presidents, others select a famous singer like Elvis, and some choose well-known sports figures or celebrities. But what person is more important than God? The Greek word for *know* here (*ginōskō*) corresponds to a deep, personal, intimate knowledge. Though God is all-powerful, all-knowing, and present everywhere, He wants to be our most intimate friend forever. Isn't that amazing?

Chapter Review Questions

1. The author offers five ways to express "radical love." What do you think about these? What does "radical love" mean to you?

2. Certainly Christ's disciples were able to love before they met Jesus. This love is repeated throughout the Old Testament. But what does Jesus mean when He says, "A *new* command I give you: Love one another. As I have loved you, so you must love one another. By this all men will know that you are my disciples, if you love one another" (John 13:34–35, emphasis added)? How is this radical love different? How is this love a "new" commandment?

3. Why is hospitality so important to the Great Commandment leader?

4. The author states, "The radical nature of forgiveness isn't simply the activity of pardoning in reaction to sins committed. It is a lifestyle of understanding." What does this statement mean to you?

5. What might be the most significant benefit of being a Great Commandment leader?

SECTION TWO

Presentia Dei

Interlude: Angels on Gun Hill

JOSH TANNER DID some soul-searching and thought back to his simpler childhood days when he'd had no responsibilities and enjoyed spending time with his family. Even church had been fun back then. He remembered some of the things he'd learned in Sunday school and wondered why his family had stopped going to church when he was a teenager. Right then, Josh decided to find a church in the neighborhood to attend the following Sunday.

When he went to church, the pastor began his sermon by proclaiming the amazing love of God found in Christ. He talked about how we can show our gratitude to God for loving us so much. Josh remembered the graduation speaker saying that we existed "to love God back." At the sermon's conclusion, the pastor asked if anyone was considering starting life over with Jesus as the Savior and Lord of his or her life. Josh felt God was calling him to put his pursuit of success, money, and even his dreams on hold to achieve his true goal in life: to live for Christ and His purposes. Josh met with the pastor after the service and made a decision to follow Jesus for the rest of his life.

Over the next few months, Josh began regularly reading the Bible and became involved in many of the church ministries. A young professional men's group met at Roosevelt Island on Saturday nights. He especially enjoyed this meeting because the guys were real and shared their hearts openly.

On one particular night, Josh experienced something remarkable. While on his way back to his apartment in Manhattan, traveling on the Sky Tram from Roosevelt Island, he sensed God opening his eyes and touching his heart.

At the exit of the Fifty-Ninth Street tram station, Josh saw a homeless man lying motionless in the middle of the sidewalk, splayed like the chalk outline of a police homicide investigation. Everyone in this posh section of Manhattan just walked on by. Josh moved closer to see if the man was dead or had just passed out. He hesitated because if he woke the homeless man from his drunken slumber, he might need to defend himself—not an exciting prospect. The homeless man's chest heaved; he was breathing.

Josh moved on. *There's nothing I can do.*

He headed toward First Avenue, where yuppies lined up to get into the hip bars and nightclubs. Limousines lined the strip's West Side. It was midnight, and the city was just getting started. As he passed O'Sullivan's Pub, a young woman burst out of the bar's door and vomited. She fell to the ground, crying. Beneath her puke-matted hair, Josh saw an attractive young lady who was utterly disgusted with herself.

He asked her if she was all right. She cursed Josh and told him to leave her alone.

Josh strolled away, embarrassed, and watched as a Rolls-Royce limousine emptied its passengers into Serendipity's, an upscale ice cream parlor on the corner. Several teenage boys hung out by the public school across the street. The fiery end of a crack pipe lit up the "Closed After Dark" sign in the public park beside the school. Another sign beside the boys announced that it was a "Drug-Free Zone."

Josh shook his head, troubled. He assumed these were probably the children of the last few working-class families still left on the Upper East Side. Eventually a fight would break out, and somebody would call the cops. Josh passed them by.

When he reached his apartment building, he smelled marijuana smoke seeping from one of the first-floor apartments. On the second floor he heard an old man crying. The man lived alone.

Now, on his floor, Josh could hear his neighbor, Charles, a paranoid schizophrenic, talking to his dead lover, who'd passed away from AIDS a few years ago. Sometimes Charles opened the hallway trash chute to talk to him, perhaps hearing his dead lover's voice in his own echo. In the morning he'd see Charles, and they'd exchange pleasantries as if nothing had happened.

Less than ten hours later, Josh went to church only a few blocks away. As Josh and the congregation sang, "I'm so glad I'm a part of the family of God," a spark of guilt smoldered in his heart.

After the service Josh took a train ride to Long Island to visit friends and spend the afternoon relaxing and barbecuing. As the train exited the tunnel that brought him out from under the East River, he glanced back at New York City. Oh, what a glorious skyline! The sun reflected magnificently off the Citicorp Center's triangle. The gargoyles on the Chrysler Building seemed to shoot rays out of their eyes. Josh relished in the fact that he lived in such a great city.

But suddenly New York City was in flames. Fire consumed the entire skyline, and Josh was overcome by fear. God was giving him a vision, he realized. Now he saw nothing out his train window but a sea of fire. The train and time seemed to be standing still.

Josh began to weep. The world was coming to an end. He was too late—he couldn't save them. Josh saw the homeless man, the crack addict, the self-abasing woman, and the schizophrenic homosexual.

They're all perishing! It's too late!

From that moment on, Josh's life was radically different. He realized that the love of God he'd experienced through his relationship with Christ was something he needed to share with others. He needed to somehow be more involved in helping others receive the love of God through Christ. Josh recalled that the church he belonged to in Manhattan was in the process of starting a new church in a poor section of the Bronx. He believed God was calling him to be part of that church plant.

Not too long after he had the vision, Josh was offered a low-level management job in the mailroom of a large hospital in the Bronx. At first he thought the job was beneath him, but he was interested in it because the hospital was located in the same neighborhood as the church plant. He talked to the pastor of the new church about possibly helping out, but the pastor said he didn't think it was good for Josh to live in Manhattan and be part of a church in the Bronx. Josh needed to do what Jesus did, he said, and become part of the community he wanted to reach.

Josh was hesitant about moving to an area with a significantly higher crime rate than most of the city. But after much prayer, he accepted the job at the hospital and moved into an apartment on Gun Hill Road in the Bronx.

After living and ministering in the Norwood section of the Bronx for over a year, the pastor of Josh's new church was discouraged. He struggled to find a way to reach the gang members on the corner near where the church met and where the pastor, his wife, and their new baby lived. The pastor told Josh that he didn't really know what to do about the gangs. The gang members ignored the pastor, or they laughed when he passed by and said hello.

Josh joined the church-planting team comprised of three couples and two other singles. They were doing well in the working-class neighborhood, offering immigrants English as a second language classes in a local bar and hosting Bible studies in their apartments. Most of the other ministries were conducted in the neighborhood streets. The fledgling new church led kids to Christ, ministered to the poor, and fed the hungry. But Josh thought the pastor wasn't really interested in reaching those in the gang because, more than anything, everyone was a little scared of them.

The pastor told the church one Sunday morning that his mother-in-law called and suggested they bake cookies and invite the gang members over. The pastor said he could hardly keep from laughing. He graciously told her, "Maybe we'll do that some day."

Later that week, Josh and the pastor attended the local police precinct's community council meeting. The pastor told the public affairs officer that their corner of Gun Hill Road was "hot" with gang activity. An officer with an attitude told Josh and the pastor that every street got "hot" during the summer. They lacked enough cops to patrol every corner.

The next night the team gathered for prayer at the pastor's apartment. While the pastor put his newborn son to sleep in his crib, multiple gun shots went off outside his apartment. Team members ducked and crouched low. When they peered out the windows, they saw Christopher Sanchez lying in a pool of blood.

At the time Josh didn't know his name but remembered his face. He was one of the corner gang members they were all afraid of but knew they somehow needed to reach for Christ. A black car sped off, and Josh and his pastor went to the scene.

The police were there in minutes. They recognized the pastor and asked if he would help control the crowd, which was mostly other gang members at that point. Josh just stood there, feeling numb from the whole experience.

When Christopher's mother showed up, the police asked her to identify Christopher's body, which still lay in the middle of the street. She wailed as she drew closer. The contents of Christopher's head had spilled onto the street; it was a gruesome site.

Several hours later Josh went home. Soaked from the constant rain and overcome by emotion, he sobbed aloud. He knew Christopher Sanchez wasn't just the drug-dealing, gang-banging menace to society everyone thought him to be. He was God's creation, originally created in His image and brutally murdered for a ten-dollar bag of marijuana.

Three days after the murder, the church was meeting in the pastor's apartment for Bible study when the buzzer rang. Over the intercom the pastor's wife asked who was there. Someone replied, "Christopher's friends." Five gang members respectfully entered the apartment. Josh and his pastor weren't afraid to see them.

The gang members said they'd seen the pastor on the street and wanted him to do a memorial service at the church for Christopher and to make sure he had a proper burial. They didn't have any money but said they were willing to get some if they needed to. The pastor agreed and asked them to return the next day.

The team decided to use some money saved in the bank to minister to the gang members. The pastor's wife baked chocolate chip cookies, and when the gang members returned, they and the pastor planned the service over milk and cookies—just like the pastor's mother-in-law had suggested.

At the memorial service the next weekend, two hundred people showed up, and over forty young people, mostly gang members, made decisions to follow Jesus Christ. The pastor challenged everyone to be peacemakers and to carry on the memory of Christopher, whose name meant "the bearer of Christ."

Chapter 4

Incarnation into Life

THE PRESENCE OF GOD

AFTER JOSH TANNER'S spiritual awakening, he learned some valuable lessons about what being a godly leader means. First, he learned we must share the gift of God's love with others for it to be fully realized. Jesus said, "It is more blessed to give than to receive" (Acts 20:35). God's gift of love to us requires regifting.

Josh also learned that the *imago Dei* must be expressed in the life of a community; leaders must be present to a group of people to show them the love of God. Just as God demonstrates His incredible love to us through His presence, so too Great Commandment leaders demonstrate their love to their followers by presenting God's love to them.

THE SPIRITUAL PRESENCE OF GOD

God not only supplies His love to us through the selfless sacrifice of His Son, Jesus Christ, on the cross but also shows us His love by always being spiritually present for us. From the beginning, God reassured His people that He would be with them. To the patriarchs, Abraham, Isaac, and Jacob, God promised to be with them when they walked in obedience to Him. Moses was especially cognizant of his need for God's loving presence. "The Lord replied, 'My Presence will go with you, and I will give you rest.' Then Moses said to him, 'If Your Presence does not go with us, do not send us up from here. How will anyone know that you are pleased with me and with your people unless you go with us? What else will distinguish me and your people from all the other people on the face of the earth?' And the Lord said to Moses, 'I will do the very thing you have asked, because I am pleased with you and I know you by name'" (Ex. 33:14–17).

The psalmist also recognized God's loving presence when he remembered how God had led Israel. "It was by your power and your strength, by the assurance of your presence, which showed that you loved them" (44:3 GNT). Furthermore, encouragement comes by knowing that God not only goes with us but also leads the way. "The Lord himself goes before you and will be with you; he will never leave you nor forsake you. Do not be afraid; do not be discouraged" (Deut. 31:8).

In addition, Jesus promises to be with us as we move forward in faith to be leaders in spreading the gospel of salvation. We can trust Jesus to be with us as we engage in His global redemptive mission because He promised to be with us "always, to the very end of the age" (Matt. 28:20). Through Christ's Spirit we are guaranteed that His presence will empower us in our mission of spreading God's love. Christ's Holy Spirit gives us the presence and power of God. "But you will receive power when the Holy Spirit comes on you; and you will be my witnesses in Jerusalem, and in all Judea and Samaria, and to the ends of the earth" (Acts 1:8).

One Greek word used to describe the Holy Spirit is *parakletos*, which literally means "called to one's side" (see John 14:16). As we walk in love (2 John 1:6), God through His Spirit walks beside us and in front of us; He also guards our rear (Ps. 139:5). He literally surrounds us with His loving presence. What a wonderful assurance we gain by knowing that God promises never to leave us to our own devices. Great Commandment leaders wholeheartedly believe that God will meet their every need and will always be with them as they lead.

God's spiritual presence is such an important part of God's ministry to all His people but especially to His leaders. Without God's tangible presence in our lives, we would lose trust in God and certainly in our own abilities. God understands that trust is built through His consistent, reliable presence and the reassurance of His love and care. King David says, "I trust in God's unfailing love" and "Blessed are those who have learned to acclaim you, who walk in the light of your presence" (Ps. 52:8; 89:15).

Trust may be the most important prerequisite for someone to follow a leader. That is why Moses begged for God's presence and cried out to Him when he was in distress. The Israelites relied on God and trusted Him for their protection and success.

We can define *trust* as having confidence in someone's ability to meet our needs—to be there for us. When we trust someone, we say that we rely on him or her to be present whenever we need him or her. Followers must be able to trust their leaders implicitly and without question. That is why Scripture promises that God will meet our every need through Christ's presence in us (Phil. 4:19; Col. 1:27).

As Great Commandment leaders put their trust in God to meet all their needs, they empty themselves of self-reliance. They are then able to draw their strength to love from the endless source of God's loving presence. God had to remind the apostle Paul of the paradox of Christ being the power and presence in his life. "But he said to me, 'My grace is sufficient for you, for my power is made perfect in weakness.' Therefore I will boast all the more gladly about my weaknesses, so that Christ's power may rest on me" (2 Cor. 12:9).

If Great Commandment leaders wish to gain the trust of others, they must resolutely and unhesitatingly put all their trust in God's promised presence and power. Walter Anderson said, "We're never so vulnerable than when we trust someone—but paradoxically, if we cannot trust, neither can we find love or joy." Trust is the basis of our faith that God is real, that His Word is true, and that His promises are reliable. Without trust in God's ongoing presence, we will be unable to flow His love to others. Again, the psalmist shows the leader the way when he prays, "May [the King] be enthroned in God's presence forever; appoint your love and faithfulness to protect him" (Ps. 61:7).

I would be remiss if I didn't mention that when we worship Christ by partaking in Holy Communion, we find yet another tangible way to encounter the spiritual presence of Jesus in our lives. Jesus gave us this sacrament as a visible sign of an inward reality and to remind us of His sacrificial and ongoing loving presence. We should never take coming to the Lord's Table lightly. Instead we should relish every opportunity to partake in the spiritual feeding of the presence of Christ through the Eucharist.

THE INCARNATION: GOD CAME TO US IN THE FLESH

How amazing is God's spiritual presence to us who believe, but even more amazing is the fact that this is not the only way God is present with us. During Old Testament times, God appeared briefly in the physical manifestation of a cloud or fire, yet no one physically saw God before Jesus came to earth because God is spirit. To behold the full glory of God the Father would have been incomprehensible, not to mention dangerous, for mere humans (Ex. 33:20). We learn in the New Testament that the only person on earth who has seen God is Jesus. "No one has ever seen God, but God the One and Only, who is at the Father's side, has made him known" (John 1:18).

How then can we fully trust in a God we cannot see? It takes faith to believe in God, and those who believe in God only through the testimony of others are called "blessed" (John 20:29). Nevertheless, God in His wisdom believed it necessary to send a deliverer in the flesh, not in the form of a sinful man like Moses but in the form of God in the flesh. Once again, God wants to demonstrate His love to us.

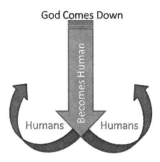

God builds trust by tangibly coming to us. He formerly spoke by His miraculous power through the prophets, but finally and ultimately He shows us His love by coming to earth in the form of His Son, Jesus Christ. "The Word became flesh and made his dwelling among us. We have seen his glory, the glory of the One and Only, who came from the Father, full of grace and truth" (John 1:14). God manifested Himself through the fully human life of Jesus, the Son of God.

Several years ago, Joan Osborne asked several questions in a song. "If God had a name, what would it be? . . .; What if God was one of us?"

Though Joan comes close to the truth in her song, God has a name. He was one of us and is one of us through the incarnation of Jesus Christ. As the great chorus says, "He came from heaven to earth to show the way!"

One day a Christian college student walked with a Hindu student to his next class. They were engaged in a cordial conversation when the Hindu student suddenly jumped. The Christian student asked the Hindu student if he was okay.

The Hindu said, "Yes, I jumped to avoid stepping on that grasshopper behind us."

"Wow! You really have respect for all living things. I wouldn't have even noticed that."

"In my religion all life has equal significance, and we believe in reincarnation." He bent down and picked up the grasshopper. "What if I were to die tomorrow and be reincarnated as a grasshopper? If I met this grasshopper, he would recognize me as the person who saved his life. He would know that I cared for him, and then he would care for me. We could become friends."

The Hindu student's story amazed the Christian student. The Christian student said, "Hey, I'm part of a club that meets tonight. Would you mind coming to our meeting? I want to tell your story to my friends."

The Hindu agreed and that evening went to the Christian student fellowship. The Christian student rose to speak and smiled at his new Hindu friend. "I want to talk tonight about grasshoppers. The Word of God says in Isaiah 40:22, '[God] sits enthroned above the circle of the earth, and its people are like grasshoppers. He stretches out the heavens like a canopy, and spreads them out like a tent to live in.'"

He told them the Hindu's story and described his idea of being reincarnated as a grasshopper to show another grasshopper that he loved it. "This is what the almighty and loving God of the universe did for us on earth," he said. "He sent His Son, Jesus Christ, to become one of us so God could show how much He loved us. The Son of God selflessly denigrated Himself to our level, took on the form of a slave, and gave up His life so we could have fellowship with God." The Hindu student was amazed and began a journey to discover who Jesus really was.

The incarnation of Christ, though perhaps not the pinnacle of Christian theology, is certainly the penultimate truth of God's plan for redeeming the world. Without the physical coming of God to earth through Jesus, there would be no transfiguration, no final sacrifice for sins, no resurrection, no ascension, no coming of the Holy Spirit, and no second coming.

The apostle John says, "That which was from the beginning, which we have heard, which we have seen with our eyes, which we have looked at and our hands have touched—this we proclaim concerning the Word of life. The life appeared; we have seen it and testify to it, and we proclaim to you the eternal life, which was with the Father and has appeared to us. We proclaim to you what we have seen and heard, so that you also may have fellowship with us. And our fellowship is with the Father and with his Son, Jesus Christ" (1 John 1:1–3).

Jesus is real! He is alive, seated at the right hand of the Father, and His Spirit lives in and through His people! Remember, God sent Jesus out of His amazing love. "For God so loved the world that he gave his one and only Son" (John 3:16; also see John 11:42; 12:44; 17:21).

Interestingly, other religions and serious historians don't usually question the fact that Jesus actually lived. God came to us in the flesh to lead us to salvation. Therefore, the incarnation becomes the model by which all leaders must lead.

LEADERS ALSO INCARNATE TO BUILD TRUST

Just as God became real flesh and blood through Jesus, so God's leaders become Jesus's real hands and feet to each subsequent generation. Christ sends them to represent Him and complete His redemptive mission. "As the Father has sent me, I am sending you" (John 20:21).

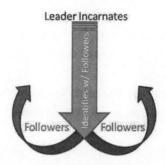

During a leadership discussion, I once mentioned to someone, "Every leader seems to be a good leader until you get to know them, and then you see their flaws, idiosyncrasies, and weaknesses." Though this statement is a generalization, there's truth in it. Though God has chosen some to lead, they aren't perfect; they are always in the process of becoming. Nevertheless, you cannot be a true leader unless followers "know" you in some tangible fashion, unless you become real to them. The notion that leaders must keep some sort of professional distance from those they lead isn't supported by Scripture. Remember, though Jesus was a successful leader, many opposed Him and chose not to follow Him.

Great Commandment leaders cannot lead or love from afar. No matter how difficult it may be to do so, they must be present to those they lead. They incarnate in a similar fashion as Jesus did. They must come down to the level of those they lead so they can gain their trust and better identify with them. Jesus led effectively because He understood exactly what we were going through. "This High Priest of ours understands our weaknesses, for he faced all of the same testings we do, yet he did not sin" (Heb. 4:15 NLT).

Like Jesus, Great Commandment leaders mingle with their followers with genuine care and lift them up. They become real to those they lead, even with all their warts, foibles, and idiosyncrasies. When Jesus came to earth, many didn't see Him as someone worthy of following. "He had no beauty or majesty to attract us to him, nothing in his appearance that we should desire him. He was despised and rejected by men, a man of sorrows, and familiar with suffering. Like one from whom men hide their faces he was despised, and we esteemed him not" (Isa. 53:2–3). Yet this same Jesus spawned a movement that now has over one billion followers.

As Great Commandment leaders care for those they lead, God's loving presence flowing from them overcomes their limitations. "No, in all these things we are more than conquerors through him who loved us" (Rom. 8:37). Incarnation is the powerful ministry of Christ's presence in His chosen leaders.

When I pastored Crestmont Alliance Church, several of our leaders were concerned about my desire for them to share in the ministry of visiting the sick in hospitals and homes (Matt. 25:35–46). One of the deaconesses felt ill equipped to do visitation because, as she said, "I never know what to say when I visit sick people in the hospital."

I replied, "Don't worry about what you'll say. The sick will just be happy that you visited them. The ministry of Christ's presence doesn't always require words."

In the management world incarnational leadership might be associated with what is called MBWA: Management by Walking Around. As service in God's kingdom, it would be called Ministry by Walking Around. It is a ministry of real presence, the incarnation of leadership. If you're not present, then you're not real, and you're not doing ministry and cannot possibly be an effective leader.

Interestingly enough, I experienced this form of incarnational leadership most intensely when I was deployed as an army chaplain in Iraq. Army chaplains, endorsed by their faith tradition, volunteer to don the uniform of those they support and serve. Like Jesus, who became human yet without sin (Heb. 4:15), army chaplains become soldiers and train like soldiers, though they are unarmed and never fight. As noncombatants, they are spiritual leaders to soldiers who bleed not only real blood but also sweat and tears. Chaplains identify with soldiers; they live with them, eat with them, and are subject to the same dangers as other soldiers. Chaplains do everything soldiers do except kill. Because of this, Army chaplains develop a special relationship with soldiers, who allow them to build a unique trust with those under their care.

This concept of incarnating oneself, of becoming Jesus to those we lead, must be contextualized to every imaginable leadership situation. Furthermore, we should not see incarnational leadership as unique to spiritual situations or contexts. We must be careful to understand that incarnation is not simply a leadership principle or theory to emulate or put into practice, expecting some return on our investment. Incarnation is much more about something we must be than something we must do. Either we're willing to incarnate in the lives of those we lead because we love them, or we're not. Therefore, the desire to incarnate should come naturally and should be an outflow of the Spirit of God as He operates in the life of the Great Commandment leader (see Gal. 5:22–23).

Chapter Review Questions

1. The author says, "the *imago Dei* must be expressed in the life of a community." What does this statement mean to you?
2. Describe some leaders in your life whom you trusted and followed. Compare them to leaders in your life you didn't trust. What primary differences exist between the two types of leaders?
3. Is trusting others easy or difficult for you? Explain.

4. What is your "trustworthiness" reputation? Do those under your authority trust you? If not, why not? What might you do differently to help build trust?
5. Do those who are your equals or colleagues trust you? If not, why not? What might you do differently to help build their trust?
6. What is incarnational leadership?

Chapter 5

Incarnation into Place

THE INCARNATION AS a core characteristic—again, not a practice—of the Great Commandment leader instructs us to become real to our followers, putting them first and becoming like them to tune in to their unique challenges and needs. When you bring yourself to the level of your followers, you gain their trust and increase your ability to lead them. If you lead with integrity and with the positive transformation of individuals, organizations, and communities in mind, your transparency will only assist you in gaining trust.

Because this premise is foundational, the next premise becomes obvious. You cannot lead from afar. God became flesh through Jesus and dwelt among His people (John 1:14). Jesus came to a specific place to do ministry. The Message brings this verse to life: "The Word became flesh and blood, and moved into the neighborhood." This is an important aspect of the incarnation. Christ not only became one of us; He lived with us where we live.

As I said before, one of the best examples of incarnation are army chaplains who go where the troops go, live where the troops live, and even risk their lives as their troops risk theirs. When I served in Iraq, a soldier in one of my companies died on another Forward Operating Base (FOB). When I received word of his death, I didn't hesitate to leave the FOB where I lived and move to the FOB where this soldier had lived. I wanted to be close to his fellow soldiers so I could minister to them. This relocation showed the soldiers in that company that I was there to live with them and show them the love of God. Living with them also gave me insights I couldn't have gained from my FOB and helped me minister to them more effectively. This simple act of moving to their FOB made a big impression on these soldiers and opened the door for effective ministry (1 Cor. 16:8–9).

You see, something about place is special to both God and humans. To the Israelites, the land was everything. The word *land* is mentioned 138 times in Genesis, 177 times in Deuteronomy, and 1,462 times throughout the Bible. To the Jewish people, the concept of land was intrinsically connected to God's love and His presence. "He will love you and bless you and increase your numbers. He will bless the fruit of your womb, the crops of your land—your grain, new wine and oil—the calves of your herds and the lambs of your flocks in the land that he swore to your forefathers to give you" (Deut. 7:13).

Yet in our increasingly transient and highly mobile modern society, we're losing a key aspect of our humanity—the connection to place. This continuing trend toward transience will make incarnational leadership more difficult. Because God puts such an important emphasis on place, however, we leaders must seriously consider how to become more attune to our followers' connectedness to a particular place.

When I was an insensitive youngster, I laughed at the jokes about people starving in other parts of the world. I asked, "Why don't they just move to where there's food and water?" In my immaturity I didn't understand the importance of place, and I progressively lost my sense of place after moving ten times before I was twenty-five. Later in life, however, I remembered my childhood in the Bronx with great fondness. I recalled sitting on stoops with neighbors, whom I thought of as aunts and uncles but really were just my parents' acquaintances. When I became older, I yearned for the deep connectedness of my youth, even in our working-class, somewhat dangerous, and impoverished neighborhood.

Therefore, incarnation isn't necessarily limited to a specific location. It's also inclusive of the connectedness people have with each other in a particular community or organization. The prophet Hosea makes this clear when he encourages the people of God. "I will plant her for myself in the land; I will show my love to the one I called 'Not my loved one.' I will say to those called 'Not my people,' 'You are my people'; and they will say, 'You are my God'" (2:23). Again, God's presence is connected to His people in a particular place.

When Great Commandment leaders understand their call to incarnational leadership, they sense that this call includes a specific group of people in a defined context. They desire to connect to these particular people at their level and in their context.

Jesus, who became flesh and blood, incarnated in a specific place to a specific people. In a surprising story from Scripture, a Canaanite woman begged for Jesus's help, but Jesus at first refused. He announced that He "was sent only to the lost sheep of Israel" (Matt. 15:24). Though Jesus helped the woman because of her great faith, He made it clear that His ministry context was focused. When He initially sent out the twelve apostles, He gave them these instructions. "Do not go among the non-Jews or enter any village of the Samaritans. Go instead to the lost sheep of Israel" (Matt. 10:5–6, author's paraphrase).

This is not to say that Jesus's ministry was limited only to the Jews because Christ gave His life for the sins of the entire world (John 3:16; Rom. 6:10; Heb. 7:27). But when He began

His ministry, His focus was on those from His own religious and ethnic background. Later, in the expanding mission of spreading the good news, the apostles took on reaching different groups of people in different places.

For the Great Commandment leader, developing an incarnational way of life isn't optional. By choosing a specific "place" to lead, the Great Commandment leader hones in on and intensely focuses on those he or she leads. This is what Jim Collins called "fierce resolve" in his book *Good to Great.* Jesus was fiercely determined to complete the singular mission God had called Him to, specifically to proclaim the gospel about Himself to the Jews in Judea. "But [Jesus] said, 'I must preach the good news of the kingdom of God to the other towns [in Judea] also, because that is why I was sent'" (Luke 4:43).

Though Jesus was providing redemption to the whole world, it was going to be given through the Jews, those deeply connected to each other in a Promised Land in accordance with a previous promise of God. "For salvation is from the Jews" (John 4:22; also see Rom. 1:16; Gal. 3:28–29).

HISTORICAL INCARNATION

The positive impact of incarnational ministry into place is well documented throughout history. Christ's chosen leaders started the church around the world, incarnating themselves among different people groups in specific places—the apostle Paul in cities throughout western Asia and Europe, the apostle Peter in Rome, and the apostle Thomas in Iraq and India, to name a few.

In modern history we have the example of Charles Wesley, who went through the poor villages of England, preaching the gospel with great success and seeing whole community transformation take root within one generation. As the men of these troubled communities converted from alcoholics, adulterers, and wife abusers into responsible, sober, loving Christian fathers and husbands, the entire village where they lived was transformed. The resulting transformation came to be known as "Redemption and Lift." As God restored families to the biblical ideal, community redemption also took place.

DEVELOPING INCARNATIONAL LEADERSHIP

When God redeems souls in a given place, the community inevitably experiences holistic redemption if those people stay. We have seen this occur in many communities in South America in the twentieth century. If redeemed, transformed individuals leave their communities, as we have seen in many places in urban and even rural America, a spiritual vacuum is left in their place. You see, incarnation must continue on through the development of multiplied, indigenous incarnational leaders. (See Chapter 10, Multiplication Paradigm.)

I was in seminary when my wife and I sensed a call to move to the Bronx to start a new church. I decided to do my master's thesis on incarnational ministry in an urban setting, using the Bronx as the area of study. One of my first tasks was to get historical and demographical data.

I called the Bronx Historical Society and spoke to a young Latina, asking her about obtaining information on the Bronx. When I told her that my wife and I were moving there in the near future, she asked me, "Where do you live now?"

I replied that I lived in Nyack just north of the city.

With a shocked tone of voice, she exclaimed, "I've been trying to get out of the Bronx for the last ten years. Why in the world would you move to the Bronx from Nyack?"

I believe the Holy Spirit prompted me to reply, "Because God so loves the Bronx!" Yes, God calls His leaders to lovingly incarnate Jesus in specific places.

As I did more research, I noted a long history of effective gospel ministry in the Bronx. The question that perplexed me was this: with all the money, all the effective church ministry, and all the good leadership in the Bronx, why had the bleak situation not improved? The reason stared me straight in the face. Though the church had done a good job of redeeming and transforming many in the Bronx, those emerging leaders inevitably left their neighborhoods for the perceived safety and comfort of the suburbs.

If transformed, indigenous leaders do not stay—are not incarnated—in their own neighborhoods, the cycle of crime, drug abuse, poverty, and broken families continues because an influx of poor and under-equipped individuals and families replaces them. Again, the incarnational leader cannot simply focus on his or her personal ministry to the lost but on incarnating God's love through the development of new generations of indigenous, incarnational leaders in every community.

URBAN IMPACT PITTSBURGH

I've been associated with several successful organizations that practiced incarnational ministry. For several years, I served as a consultant with Urban Impact, a wonderful incarnational ministry led by Rev. Dr. Ed Glover. When Ed and his wife, Tammy, arrived in Pittsburgh's North Side to serve as youth ministers, the church God had called them to was struggling. The community had changed. Though many African-Americans had moved in, the church remained all white.

Pastor Ed and Tammy realized their work with youth needed to include all members of the community. They decided to move into the neighborhood and work with African-American kids. Ed and Tammy incarnated themselves into the lives of the young people of a specific place. Though they endured great hardship, ultimately the gospel was effective in transforming not only the people of that section of the North Side but also the place itself. When Ed and Tammy bought their home, over

50 percent of the houses on their block were boarded up and unoccupied. Within just a few years, redeemed and transformed local people moved in, and today the street is a beacon of hope. The church, Allegheny Center Alliance Church, was also transformed. It grew from a congregation of about five hundred whites to a church of over three thousand, with almost a third being African-Americans from the North Side.

ALIQUIPPA IMPACT

In 2004 God called my wife, Martha, and me to pastor Crestmont Alliance Church in Hopewell, Pennsylvania, just outside Pittsburgh. Before I arrived at the church, Joel Repic, a young, vibrant college student and member of the church, called to ask if I had a vision for incarnational ministry. I told him I did, and thus began our conversations about starting an outreach ministry to Aliquippa, one of the most distressed communities in America.

Joel began Aliquippa Impact with Crestmont's full support, a few thousand dollars, and a handful of joy-filled Toccoa Falls College students. Joel and his radical college friends knew that if they were going to help redeem and transform the poor and primarily African-American community in Aliquippa, they needed to live among them. A drive-by ministry could never build trust. In its first year, Aliquippa Impact secured housing for all the student ministers in downtown Aliquippa, and the entire ministry was conducted in the community.

Two years after they began the ministry, Joel and his wife, Chelsea, bought a house in one of the poorest sections of the city. Like a pied piper, they led many more Toccoa Falls graduates to incarnate there as well. It took some time for them to build trust in the community, but they've led many families to saving faith in Jesus and are beginning to transform the entire city for Christ.

The success of Urban Impact Pittsburgh, Aliquippa Impact, and other holistic ministries like them is contingent on leaders incarnating themselves into the lives of a particular people in a particular place and developing indigenous leaders from within the community.

Great Commandment leaders recognize that God wants every community transformed, and the only way to incarnate into a certain group of people is to move into their context and live life with them, developing a new generation of indigenous, incarnational leaders.

Chapter Review Questions

1. Incarnational ministry requires Great Commandment leaders to live among the people they serve. How does this requirement challenge your understanding of leadership?
2. What are the pros and cons of incarnational ministry?
3. The author's teaching on "incarnation into place" invites us to see where we do ministry as holy. How does envisioning our ministry environment as a holy place inform our service?

4. What are some ways a Great Commandment leader might transform a community?

5. Chapter 5 provides many models of incarnational ministry and leadership. Which models do you most identify with? What type of model might best work in your unique context?

Chapter 6

Incarnation into Service

I'VE HEARD IT said many times that God loves us just because we are His creation, but because He loves us so much, He would never leave us in our current sinful condition. He wants to change us back into His perfect image (Matt. 5:48). Therefore, when Jesus began preaching, His favorite term was "Repent!" (Matt. 4:17). *Repentance* simply means to change (Greek: *metanoia*), a change that is inclusive of all our thoughts, desires, and actions. To "repent" literally means to turn from the way we are going and move in a new direction, into a new way of living. For us it means turning completely away from sin and turning our lives over to God in complete submission to Christ.

When God was incarnated into flesh in a specific place and time, He was also changed radically—not from a sinner, for Jesus was without sin (Heb. 4:15), but from the all-powerful God to a voluntary human slave. Amazingly, the God who created us and has dominion over us also came to serve us. This concept is extremely hard to wrap our minds around, so the Bible expounds on this critical truth. "[Jesus], being in very nature God, did not consider equality with God something to be grasped, but made himself nothing, taking the very nature of a servant, being made in human likeness. And being found in appearance as a man, he humbled himself and became obedient to death—even death on a cross!" (Phil. 2:6–8).

When God came in human flesh, He not only took on our humanity but also amazingly came to serve humanity. Christ veiled His divine nature and came not as an upper-class nobleman but as an innocent babe totally dependent on His parents and then an adult stooping down to be a bondservant (Isa. 52:2–3). It seems preposterous, but it's true: Jesus became a slave so He could give His life as a ransom for all.

For years many have studied the above verses in Philippians, a passage that even has its own theological term: *kenosis*. But Christ not only voluntarily became a servant to those He led but also continually showed His servanthood throughout His ministry on earth.

In an awe-inspiring, surprising scene immediately before His betrayal, Jesus took off His outer garment and washed the dirty, smelly feet of His followers, including His betrayer.

> Jesus knew that the Father had put all things under his power, and that he had come from God and was returning to God; so he got up from the meal, took off his outer clothing, and wrapped a towel around his waist. After that, he poured water into a basin and began to wash his disciples' feet, drying them with the towel that was wrapped around him.... [Jesus said,] "You call me 'Teacher' and 'Lord,' and rightly so, for that is what I am. Now that I, your Lord and Teacher, have washed your feet, you also should wash one another's feet. I have set you an example that you should do as I have done for you."
>
> —John 13:3–5, 13–15

Of course, the apostle Peter protested this seeming travesty of decorum, as I'm sure we all would have. What kind of leader would stoop down to wash his or her followers' dirty feet? What kind of omnipotent king rides into town on a lowly donkey (Matt. 21:1–11)? What kind of Savior allows His own subjects to beat, humiliate, and crucify Him? The God-man and servant, Jesus Christ, that's who!

This lesson is essential to the Great Commandment leader. Confident of the love of God, we can move from self-aggrandizement to sacrificially serving others to build them up. Notice the wording in the above passage. Knowing that He was God's beloved Son and having complete confidence in that loving relationship, Jesus had no problem submitting Himself to those who were clearly lower than Him for the purposes of serving God. Great Commandment leaders in their own humility will do the same.

Jesus's incarnation shows us that we also need to be radically changed into servants. Our attitudes should be like Christ's (Phil. 2:5), and we shouldn't consider that all the authority and power Christ has given His chosen leaders (Matt 28:18) are things we should exercise for our own benefit. Instead we should become servants to those we lead. We must put aside our selfish desires and, like Jesus, become slaves to others. The apostle Paul repeated this message. "Do nothing out of selfish ambition or vain conceit, but in humility consider others better than yourselves. Each of you should look not only to your own interests, but also to the interests of others" (Phil. 2:3–4).

Incarnation implies a radical internal change.

TRUE SERVANTHOOD

I remember attending an urban church planters' conference in Queens, New York. My instructors posed a poignant question about the incarnation. "Why did Jesus come to earth?"

Some of the participants answered, "To seek and save the lost," "To die for the sins of the world," or "To preach the gospel."

Our trainer said, "You're all right, but you're missing something fundamental."

One participant said, "Jesus came to do the will of His Father in heaven."

"Exactly!" the trainer shouted. He quoted this important truth from Jesus: "For I have come down from heaven not to do my will but to do the will of him who sent me" (John 6:38). To be a church leader or any kind of leader in God's kingdom, we must understand what it means to be a servant of Christ and others—to be incarnated into the service of God.

When Jesus wasn't calling the world to repentance, He was commanding us to go after Him. Jesus drew a line in the sand and called us to a decision. "Follow me," He said (Matt. 4:19; 8:22; 9:9; 10:38; 16:24; 19:21). When Christ says we should follow Him, we learn from Scripture that Jesus intends to be our Master. Jesus is "Lord of lords and King of kings!" (Rev. 17:14). Just as Jesus became completely obedient to God the Father, so are we to be completely obedient to Jesus. In His final words before His ascension, Christ tells His disciples to continue the mission of making Jesus followers by "teaching them to *obey* everything I have commanded you" (Matt. 28:20, emphasis added). God calls us to obedience. God wants us to love Him back by being obedient to Him!

The fact is, the Bible in its original language doesn't call us to be "servants" of Jesus; instead, it calls us to be slaves of Him who called us. In his book *The Gospel According to Jesus*, John MacArthur correctly laments that most modern translations of the English Bible avoid the literal translation of the word *servant* from its original meaning of "slave" (Greek: *doulos*). MacArthur says, "The idea of a Christian as a slave and Christ as Master is almost totally missing from the vocabulary of contemporary evangelical Christianity."[6] Nevertheless, even if you used one of the correctly translated New Testament words for *servant* (deacon; Greek: *diakonos*), you would find that at its root is a lowly kind of menial table service, not some glorious leadership position.

To fully become a Great Commandment leader, we must understand what being a voluntary slave of Jesus means. First, slaves do only what their master tells them. The apostle Paul instructs earthly slaves in their relationships with their masters. "Obey them not only to win their favor when their eye is on you, but like slaves of Christ, doing the will of God from your heart" (Eph. 6:6).

Second, Jesus says we cannot serve two masters. We must serve Him and His purposes only, just as Christ served the purposes and commands of His Father in heaven. And third, if we are not slaves to Christ, we are slaves to sin. But the apostle Paul says that, as we are in Christ, we are no longer slaves to sin because "you have been set free from sin and have become slaves to righteousness" (Rom. 6:18).

Amazingly, this slavery to righteousness is indeed the truest form of freedom. "It is for freedom that Christ has set us free. Stand firm, then, and do not let yourselves be burdened again by a yoke of slavery" (Gal. 5:1). To no longer be subject to a "yoke of slavery," Great Commandment leaders will voluntarily submit themselves totally to Christ. The paradox of the incarnation spurs even more paradoxes. Maybe the clearest way to understand this concept is by revisiting an Old Testament story.

According to Mosaic law, no Israelites were allowed to keep fellow Jews as slaves for more than six years. In the seventh year, they had to set their Jewish slaves free. "But if the servant declares, 'I love my master…and do not want to go free,' then his master must take him before the judges. He shall take him to the door or the doorpost and pierce his ear with an awl. Then he will be his servant for life" (Ex. 21:5–6). Just as Jesus was pierced for our transgressions, taking our sins upon Himself (Isa. 53:5), so we too, as followers of Master Jesus, allow ourselves to be spiritually pierced, dying to self, to identify ourselves as slaves of righteousness. Again, we should note that this lowering of self should be done out of our love and gratitude to God in keeping with the Great Commandment.

THE SERVANT LEADERSHIP PARADOX

So how is it that we can ever become "leaders" if we are constantly expected to serve God and those we are supposed to lead? Furthermore, the challenge of incarnational servant leadership becomes even more paradoxical because Jesus clearly says we shouldn't call anyone "leaders; for One is your Leader, that is, Christ" (Matt. 23:10 NASB). Also, because the role of a teacher is a leadership function, especially in the church, the apostle James said, "Not many of you should presume to be teachers, my brothers, because you know that we who teach will be judged more strictly" (James 3:1).

And if that doesn't muddy the waters enough, we read the paradoxical story of the last being first. "[Jesus and the apostles] came to Capernaum. When [Jesus] was in the house, he asked them, 'What were you arguing about on the road?' But they kept quiet because on the way they had argued about who was the greatest. Sitting down, Jesus called the Twelve and said, 'If anyone wants to be first, he must be the very last, and the servant of all'" (Mark 9:33–35).

The key to sorting out the servant leadership paradox is humility. Great Commandment leaders humble themselves as Jesus did (Phil. 2:8) so God will supernaturally empower them to lead obediently. Ironically, Jim Collins "discovered" the solution to this paradox in his research when he reported in *Good to Great* that the key difference distinguishing great leaders from merely good ones was the great leader's paradoxical combination of both humility and fierce resolve. The great leaders in Collins's study weren't flashy, media-loving, charismatic types. Instead, the "great" leaders were quietly strong, persistent, focused, giving others the credit when things went right, and taking the blame when they went wrong.[7] Therefore, it shouldn't be surprising when Jesus says that "whoever exalts himself will be humbled, and whoever humbles himself will be exalted" (Matt. 23:12).

As the apostle Paul says, slaves ought to willingly and humbly obey what their masters tell them to do (Eph. 6:5–6). Likewise, the Great Commandment leader in humility accepts God's calling to obediently serve as a leader under the authority of Christ. We do so because we love God and those we have incarnated to serve. Paul reiterates that servant leadership is a calling. "Be shepherds of God's flock that is under your care, serving as overseers—not because you must, but because you are willing, as God wants you to be; not greedy for money, but eager to serve; not lording it over those entrusted to you, but being examples to the flock" (1 Peter 5:2–3). The people we are shepherds of are those we must care for.

From the verse above we clearly understand that God has called us to serve as leaders, not to lead others to serve us. How much different we are to be than those who believe leadership comes with its privileges. "Jesus called them together and said, 'You know that the rulers of the Gentiles lord it over them, and their high officials exercise authority over them. Not so with you. Instead, whoever wants to become great among you must be your servant, and whoever wants to be first must be your slave—just as the Son of Man did not come to be served, but to serve, and to give his life as a ransom for many'" (Matt. 20:25–28).

God calls Great Commandment leaders to be servants of God and of those they lead. Nevertheless, they must answer the call to leadership when it comes.

In Table 2 on the next page, I have provided a brief taxonomy of leadership positions described in the New Testament. We can find the spiritual or moral qualifications for these positions in 1 Timothy 3, but all of them are based on callings and

God's giftings. I have also included some non-church-based equivalents because the majority of Christian leaders do not work in vocational ministry.

Table 2: Leadership Roles of Christians in God's Kingdom

Ancient Church Position	Modern Church Position	Non-Church-Based Equivalent
Apostle	Church Planter/ Missionary	Entrepreneur
Prophet	Itinerant Church Preacher	Activist/Politician
Evangelist	Evangelist	Consultant
Pastor	Pastor/Chaplain	Counselor/Psychologist
Teacher	Teacher/Professor	Teacher/Professor
Overseer/Bishop	Elder	Vice President/ Department Director
Deacon	Deacon/Deaconess	Social Service Provider
Administrator	Executive/ Administrative Pastor	Manager

The apostle Paul says that if anyone "sets his heart on being an overseer, he desires a noble task" (1 Tim. 3:1). The fact is, God is calling many people into Christian leadership. In the church the elder role is a position each adult male congregant should aspire to in his development as a man of God. However, the official position, it should be understood, is open only to those whom God has called. Nonetheless, those who want to do the will of God will prepare themselves for the task of being humble servant leaders under the headship of Christ.

Finally, please remember that *love* is an action word, not simply an emotion. Therefore, Great Commandment leaders will use their calling, gifting, and resources to demonstrate the love of God to those they lead. "For God so loved the world that he gave" (John 3:16). Incarnation into life, place, and service is a process of loving God and others, and we accomplish it by living life with those we serve as leaders.

Chapter Review Questions

1. What role does repentance play in the character formation of a Great Commandment leader?
2. How does the teaching that God became human inform our understanding of Christian leadership?
3. In John 13 we read the story of Jesus washing the feet of His apostles. How might this story serve as an essential model for Great Commandment leaders?
4. The author presents a taxonomy of leadership positions. What might we learn about Great Commandment leadership from these positions?
5. According to the author, we best understand the servant leadership paradox by the paradoxical combination of humility and fierce resolve. How does this position inform your understanding of leadership?

SECTION THREE
Missio Dei

Interlude: The Road Less Traveled

NOT LONG AFTER the memorial service for Christopher Sanchez, the new church in the Bronx experienced significant growth and moved out of the pastor's home to a storefront off Gun Hill Road. The pastor invited Josh Tanner to assist him in looking at potential sites for the church to move to when the attendance grew more. During one of the site visits, the pastor asked Josh if he would consider becoming the first elder of their new church. The pastor said, "I have noticed your humility and your desire to be part of God's plan to redeem the lost and transform the world for Christ." After some time in prayer and study of God's Word, Josh humbly accepted the leadership role.

At the hospital, besides running an efficient mail distribution operation, Josh worked with a lot of young people in the mailroom—mostly young adults from the neighborhood. He helped some to get their GEDs. He walked some through the process of getting into college and taught a few how to drive. Everyone in the department loved Josh, and he was often invited to parties in the homes of his employees and their families.

During his tenure as mailroom supervisor, he led twelve of his staff to the Lord. Over forty people attending the new church were employees of the hospital where Josh worked, and he was responsible for inviting every one of them.

During lunch once a week, Josh also led a growing Bible study that was about to branch off into a second Bible study on a different day. The leader of the new Bible study would be one of the young mailroom workers Josh had led to the Lord. Lives were being redeemed and transformed in the Bronx.

Because Josh was so successful at leading so many to the Lord, the pastor asked him to train the church's members to develop a heart for the lost and a lifestyle of personal evangelism. Josh first taught the church members the truth of God's love, showing them how they could love the things God loves. He used John 3:16 as the basis for a thirteen-week evangelism course to train others on living life as Christ's ambassadors throughout the world.

Over the next few years, the church multiplied to over five hundred people. They increased the number of outreaches to the community, and they started a new congregation in the adjoining neighborhood.

Violence significantly decreased in the area where Christopher was killed. Once five to seven murders per year were not unusual in that section of the Bronx, but in the two years since Christopher's death, not one person had been murdered in that neighborhood. Violence had decreased across the board. The police gave some credit to the church Josh was part of.

Josh's superiors also noticed his leadership as a mailroom supervisor at the hospital. About a year and half after Josh arrived at the hospital, the vice president of personnel asked Josh to become assistant director for hospital admissions.

Though Josh earned enough money to move out of the neighborhood, he didn't. He felt like he was an integral member of his community. He'd invested a lot of God's love into a lot of people, and leaving wasn't an option. Josh knew God was going to do something even bigger in that section of the Bronx; in fact, he felt that God wanted to redeem and transform the entire community.

After seeing his potential for taking on even more leadership responsibilities, Josh's new supervisor suggested that he enroll in a master's program in hospital administration; the hospital would even pay for the degree. Josh took his boss's advice and enrolled in the program at a local college the following September.

One of the first classes Josh was required to take was Diversity in the Workplace. Part of the class requirements was to do a field study in the students' workplace to determine the diversity "climate" of the organization. Each student needed to develop a systematic way of studying how people of different ethnicities, genders, and age groups were treated in their work environments.

As assistant director of admissions at the hospital, one of Josh's responsibilities was to find ways to decrease the time each patient needed to wait before a provider saw him or her. Josh had been involved in an ongoing wait-time study, so he decided to see if wait times varied by ethnicity, gender, or age. In addition, Josh had access to the department's security cameras and admissions data on each patient. He anticipated finding that his hospital, already known for its diverse workforce, would do well on the climate survey.

Unfortunately, what Josh discovered was disappointing, and the evidence was staggering. After assembling clear statistical evidence, Josh identified that blacks, women, and the elderly consistently waited much longer to be seen than whites, Hispanics, males, and those under fifty-five years old. In addition, only 5 percent of the admissions personnel were black; the rest were Hispanic, Asian, or white. He struggled with writing up the findings for his class because he knew he had the responsibility to report them to the director.

When Josh met with the director about the issue, the director told him to fix the problem himself and said the data wasn't going to the vice president of hospital affairs. Josh protested, saying that the problem was systemic and needed to be addressed at the highest levels of the organization. By the end of the conversation, however, it was clear to Josh that he risked losing his job if he revealed the data to the vice president.

Later that night, conflicted and confused, Josh read Scripture, which reminded him that God was a God of love and justice. Like a bright light shining on the text, the psalmist spoke to him. "The Lord loves righteousness and justice; the earth is full of his unfailing love" (Ps. 33:5).

Chapter 7

Transformation

GREAT COMMANDMENT LEADERSHIP PRACTICE

JOSH'S EXCEPTIONAL NEW leadership abilities didn't come from the knowledge acquired while studying leadership in college or from his ancestor's genetic traits. No, the amazing love he'd received from God supernaturally empowered him for effective leadership, and he began to understand what being a leader meant from the examples of Jesus Christ and the apostles. In addition, he learned how to serve in an incarnational manner from his pastor. By allowing the love of God to flow from him to others, Josh was being transformed into the image of his Creator and beginning to transform those around him.

This is the transformation God had in mind even before He created the world. God's plan is to use His transformed people to help transform others. The apostle Paul reminds us that those who are in Christ are His ambassadors "created in Christ Jesus to do good works, which God prepared in advance for us to do" (Eph. 2:10). Josh was simply carrying out the work of love God had created for him to accomplish.

Like Jesus, Great Commandment leaders show their love for God by completing the mission God has prepared for them (*missio Dei*). They should be able to say the words of Jesus with confidence. "I have brought you glory on earth by completing the work you gave me to do" (John 17:4). The mission God has given every Great Commandment leader is the transformation of individuals, groups, and whole communities. God wants all people everywhere to be redeemed and transformed back into the *imago Dei* (2 Peter 3:9). This transformation process in Christian circles is most often times called "discipleship" because it is the process of making followers of Christ. God's transformational process is designed to restore people back to a right relationship with Him.

TRANSFORMATIONAL LEADERSHIP

What is transformation? How should we understand it? The apostle Paul states that all believers should no "longer conform to the pattern of this world, but be transformed [Greek: *metamorphoo*] by the renewing of your mind[s]" (Rom. 12:2). When we practice repentance (Greek: *metanoia*), changing our attitudes and beliefs about who Jesus is and what He wants us to do, and when we receive the love God has for us in Jesus, we will be transformed from focusing on the concerns of this world to the priorities of God and His kingdom. Great Commandment leaders are those whom God has chosen to transform others after having begun their own transformation process.

This notion of being a transformational leader isn't new. From the times of the patriarchs, God has expected all His people to be transformative agents in the world (Gen. 12:2–3; Ps. 67). Jesus is the greatest example of the transformational leader. He lived life among those He was transforming. He served them, taught and trained them, healed those who were sick, and ultimately gave His life for them. Transformation begins and ends with Jesus.

Interestingly, many leadership scholars today are "discovering" transformational leadership. Transformational leaders, according to Bernard Bass, act as role models, inspiring others to be and do more than they thought possible; they provide individual attention and care, encouraging their followers to do things in new ways.[8] Peter Northouse reports that transformational leaders are able to get others to desire change and motivate them to improve. How do these leaders do that? Northouse says that transformational leaders assess the desires of their followers, satisfy their needs, and value each follower personally.[9] Isn't it wonderful when secular researchers "discover" the deep truths of God?

For Great Commandment leaders the transformation process is accomplished by teaching others to be obedient to God, primarily through the proclamation of the gospel, personal example, spiritual formation, and godly service so God can transform those they lead back into the loving image of God. The end goal of Great Commandment leaders is to help people be transformed into the image of Jesus Christ. "And we, who with unveiled faces all reflect the Lord's glory, are being transformed into his likeness with ever-increasing glory, which comes from the Lord, who is the Spirit" (2 Cor. 3:18).

Though leadership success naturally comes from sharing Christ's love, every Great Commandment leader desires to develop the leadership gifts and abilities God has given to him or her (see 1 Cor. 14:12; Matt. 25:14–30). God's leaders also need to be continually transformed by renewing their minds and developing their leadership craft.

TRANSFORMATIONAL LEADERSHIP PARADIGMS

One way we can develop ourselves as leaders is to discover and practice the models or patterns of loving leadership Jesus and the apostles practiced as they transformed lives. These models or patterns are sometimes called "paradigms." Paradigms can be the conceptual framework used to understand and execute a particular practice.

In the next few chapters, we will introduce six transformational leadership paradigms that assist us as we practice Great Commandment leadership. All these leadership paradigms are based on God's Word and practiced by Christ, the apostles, and other godly leaders in Scripture.

We've left these practices in the last section of this book because we needed to first emphasize that the practice of Great Commandment leadership can occur only subsequently to becoming Great Commandment leaders. Only after we've appropriated the love of God and begun to operate as willing vessels for Christ's love to others can we begin to work on developing these critical leadership skills.

The six critical transformational leadership paradigms for Great Commandment leaders are the following: (1) the equipping paradigm, (2) the coaching paradigm, (3) the multiplication paradigm, (4) the outcome paradigm; (5) the justice paradigm; and (6) the "glocal" paradigm. These six Great Commandment transformational leadership paradigms are integrated models for leadership—that is, they work together simultaneously. However, we can use each for different purposes or situations. For example, the first two paradigms, though foundational, are primarily designed for use with individuals or small groups. We can use the next two with organizations, and the last two can apply to the wider community.

The Great Commandment leader, who is empowered by Christ's Spirit, will instinctively assess when a particular paradigm works best in a given situation with different followers. Scriptural truth is the basis for all these paradigms, but we may not easily and intuitively integrate them into a seamless, functional whole. Though many leaders might discover these leadership paradigms in their study of Scripture, they may need to develop their use and learn how to integrate them for maximum effect. In the next six chapters, we will discuss each paradigm, its scriptural basis, and how it works to transform individuals, organizations, and/ or the wider community.

Chapter Review Questions

1. What does transformation mean to you? What areas of your life need to be transformed so you can become a more effective leader?
2. How is the transformational process accomplished in the Great Commandment leader?
3. What is the ultimate goal of the transformational leader?
4. The author introduces six transformational leadership paradigms. What lessons might we learn from having so many different models?
5. What is the relationship between repentance and transformation? How does it inform personal leadership development?

Chapter 8

Equipping Paradigm

LEADERSHIP THROUGH EQUIPPING

THE FIRST TRANSFORMATIONAL leadership practice we will examine is the equipping paradigm. The primary work of the Great Commandment leader is to equip others to become participants in God's mission (Ex. 18:20; Matt. 28:18–20; 1 Tim. 3:2; 2 Tim. 2:2). Regardless of what you want to call him—teacher, trainer, mentor, coach, equipper, or instructor—this is the practical call of leadership according to Scripture. God calls and empowers leaders to serve others by equipping them for service in His kingdom.

The Great Commandment leader focuses on three key areas to equip others for the mission to which God has called all of us. We transform followers by (1) imparting truth (transforming minds), (2) helping them to develop godly character (transforming hearts), and (3) assisting them in gaining practical skills to fulfill their unique calling in life (transforming wills).

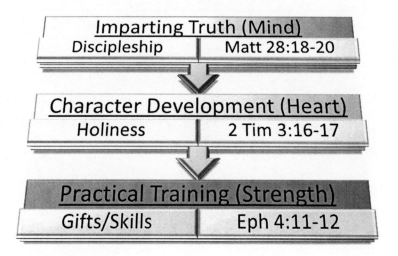

Imparting Truth

God has called every Christian to make disciples—that is, to make followers of Jesus. As servant leaders of Christ, our mission is to make followers of Jesus, not followers of us (Matt. 23:8). In the Great Commission, wherever God calls the leader to go, He will "make disciples" (Greek: *mathēteuō*) of Jesus and "[teach] [Greek: *didasko*] them to obey" the truths Jesus commanded (Matt. 28:19–20).

When we received our ultimate freedom in Christ (Gal. 5:1), we learned that real freedom comes from the knowledge that Jesus is the embodiment of all truth. The Bible says that truth comes from Jesus (John 1:17) and that everything that is good and true is found in Jesus. "I am the way and the truth and the life. No one comes to the Father except through me" (John 14:6).

Throughout the Gospels, Jesus began His most poignant teaching with the phrase "I tell you the truth." Truth matters deeply to God, and imparting truth is the first work of equipping disciples. To be effective leaders in God's eyes, we must lead people away from the untruths of the Devil, the father of lies (John 8:44), the deception of wayward men (2 Tim. 4:3), and the sinful temptations of our own flesh (Rom. 1:25–32). We will transform our followers' minds, first and foremost, by leading them into the truth of God's Word (Rom. 12:1).

Jesus said we would know the truth when we understood and followed the commands of His Word (John 8:32). That truth is what frees us from sin and transforms us into godly leaders. Jesus prayed that we would be "[sanctified] by the truth; your word is truth" (John 17:17). It should be abundantly clear by now that before a person can be a Great Commandment leader, his or her knowledge of Scripture must be fairly developed, for one cannot impart to others truth one has not received for himself or herself.

Unfortunately, the notion of truth is under attack throughout the world through the postmodern movement and among Christians who no longer find truth to be of paramount importance. George Barna recently noted that less than 20 percent of self-described, born-again Christians have a worldview informed by the truth of Scripture.[10] Our Western educational systems are far more interested in teaching the truths of science, math, and language arts than what God says is most important.

Yet this hasn't always been the case. In ancient Israel most of the young men committed the entire body of Scripture to memory. But if you asked young people today what Scripture says on life's most important topics, you'd sadly find that most are completely ignorant of such matters. Great Commandment leaders are different; they love God's Word and like David delight "in the law of the Lord, and on his law…[meditate] day and night" (Ps. 1:2). Because they want to be effective leaders in God's kingdom, they immerse themselves in the truth of God's Word.

The essence of knowing God is having a correct understanding of who He is and what He expects from His followers. We cannot know God and His redemptive plan apart from His revelation in His Word. The Great Commandment leader is commissioned to share the truth of an amazingly loving God and His plan for the salvation of all people through Jesus Christ. This is what Jesus called the "good news." God commands each of us to proclaim the reality that Jesus is the ultimate truth, the Savior of the world.

However, this proclamation doesn't mean God has called all of us to be full-time ministers or missionaries. Grave error exists in the minds of many in the church that only the paid clergy are responsible for discipleship training and equipping. Everyone called to leadership should be involved in the process of equipping others for godly living and completing Christ's mission, whether volunteers or paid leaders. The first part of that call is understanding the truth and teaching it correctly to others. The apostle Paul admonishes all leaders to "do [their] best to present [themselves] to God as one approved, a workman who does not need to be ashamed and who correctly handles the word of truth" (2 Tim. 2:15).

Those called to be leaders shouldn't consider this directive to be a burden. Many leadership scholars point out that leaders tend to have high levels of intelligence and a strong passion for knowledge. That doesn't mean they necessarily excel in academics, but they have a deep thirst for the truth. Great Commandment leaders have an intense desire to know the truth of God's Word and to communicate it to others. As I noted in Chapter 2, the secret to real success is knowledge of God's Word, and that success is contingent on sharing the truth found in it (Josh. 1:8). Therefore, the primary interaction Great Commandment leaders will have with those they lead is to impart the truth of God's Word.

Training in Righteousness

The second area of equipping the Great Commandment leader focuses on is training in righteousness. "All Scripture is God-breathed and is useful for teaching, rebuking, correcting and training in righteousness, so that the man of God may be thoroughly equipped for every good work" (2 Tim. 3:16–17). By using God's Word as the basis for moral and ethical training, followers of Jesus will learn how to live godly lives. Since the leader's character is critical to building trust, righteousness is a prerequisite for being a good leader. How we live speaks volumes to those who'll follow our example. Moral shortcomings or ethical lapses will severely inhibit a leader's ability to lead.

The apostle Paul says that the Scriptures are useful to teach and correct wrong thinking, attitudes, and actions. We should use all Scripture to instruct ourselves and others in holiness. The point is that we won't be able to do Jesus's good work unless we are "thoroughly equipped." The Greek word here (*artios*) means we are made complete or perfected for God's work. God's Word refines us so we can be made complete in Jesus. The Word of God is a living, dynamic word that acts as a sword, penetrating "soul and spirit, joints and marrow; it judges the thoughts and attitudes of the heart" (Heb. 4:12).

The apostle Paul reminds leaders to "proclaim him, admonishing and teaching everyone with all wisdom, so that we may present everyone perfect in Christ" (Col. 1:28). The call to teach or preach the gospel is God's highest call (Rom. 10:15; Eph. 4:11-14). The teacher/preacher's job is to instruct followers to become perfect. This is a lofty goal, but the objective of Great Commandment leadership is that followers of Jesus would be transformed into the perfect, loving image of God. Is the bar set too high? No. Jesus told us, "Be perfect, therefore, as your heavenly Father is perfect" (Matt. 5:48).

Thankfully, God assures us of His care and that He will supernaturally work to transform us. The apostle Paul prayed confidently that "he who began a good work in you will carry it on to completion until the day of Christ Jesus" (Phil. 1:6). The work of becoming holy (complete, perfect) is a lifelong process, so the aim isn't instant perfection but long-term transformation. The Great Commandment leader lovingly transforms others spiritually and ethically by training them according to God's holy Word. The apostle John reminds us, "But if anyone obeys his Word, God's love is truly made complete in him. This is how we know we are in him: Whoever claims to live in him must walk as Jesus did" (1 John 2:5–6). We teach those entrusted to us to be obedient to Christ's command to walk in holiness.

Equipping the Saints

When listing the leadership functions of the church, the apostle Paul emphatically states that these ministries are for leaders under Christ to use to equip others for the work of serving Christ. "This is why it says: 'When he ascended on high, he led captives in his train and gave gifts to men.'…It was he who gave some to be apostles, some to be prophets, some to be evangelists, and some to be pastors and teachers, to prepare God's people for works of service, so that the body of Christ may be built up until we all reach unity in the faith and in the knowledge of the Son of God and become mature, attaining to the whole measure of the fullness of Christ" (Eph. 4:8, 11–13).

In Chapter 6 I briefly explained the five-fold ministry of Christian leadership, but the emphasis should never be on the offices themselves but on the functional goal—"to prepare God's people for works of service." Other Bible versions use the word *equip* (Greek: *katartismos)* instead of *prepare* to describe this important function in completing God's redemptive mission on earth.

As an equipper, the Great Commandment leader isn't necessarily a job trainer but a facilitator who ensures that each person develops his or her unique gifts and abilities for use in building God's kingdom. At the church my wife attended before we were married, all the ministerial staff were appropriately called "equipping pastors." God-called leaders must see their primary function as building up those they lead.

One reason the Great Commandment leader can only facilitate the equipping of others is because God uniquely created every person on earth. God loves variety. He made every person different so we could each accomplish the unique work "God prepared in advance for us to do" (Eph. 2:10). Therefore, God charges leaders with assisting each person they lead to fulfill his or her destiny in Christ. We will not be made complete in Christ until each of us does exactly what God designed us to do. That's why it's so important that leaders see their function not as those in charge but as those who serve others by building them up and equipping them.

The Bible lists many different functions necessary for both church and society, including administrators, teachers, assistants (servants), counselors, craftsmen, businessmen, artists, healing professionals, and many others. Every believer should serve Christ with the gifts and talents God has given him or her; the leader is the primary agent to assist believers in the development of those gifts and abilities. Again, it isn't that leaders are involved in specific on-the-job training, but where leaders are equipped, they will transfer that wisdom and knowledge to those they lead. Great Commandment leaders provide guidance, encouragement, and resources to those they lead so they become mature in their development.

Pedagogical Method

Integrating these three equipping functions—imparting truth, training in righteousness, and empowering for service—

into a seamless, natural process requires creating a usable teaching method (pedagogy). When Jesus was on earth, He used a specific method of equipping we can adapt into our modern context.

Now, you might be asking yourself, why don't we just do exactly what Jesus did if He is the perfect example? Though this question may seem intuitive, it's problematic because our educational culture is much more varied and complex now than it was during the time of Jesus. For example, in ancient times most disciples of rabbinical teachers lived with their instructors and followed them wherever they went. Today, however, Western society is more fragmented. Teachers are not expected to live with their students, nor do they spend all their time with them.

Nevertheless, we can translate four overarching ancient principles Jesus used into a modern framework. The four methods Jesus used and taught to his disciples are (1) modeling desired behavior while teaching with varied approaches, (2) working alongside others during a cooperative activity, (3) sending them out on trial runs, and (4) sending them forth prepared and equipped for their own specific mission.

First, Jesus modeled the kinds of behaviors and attitudes He wanted His followers to emulate. Someone said that the best kind of teaching is caught rather than taught. Rather than simply depending on a lecture method, Jesus often followed a particular action with a didactic lesson (Matt. 12:22–37). This combination of a modeled action followed by an explanation is as effective today as it was during Jesus's day.

Jesus also used real-life stories and situations through parables to illustrate His main teaching point. Sometimes He used object lessons to drive home an important axiom. Matthew 22:17–22 is a good example. "'Tell us then, what is your opinion? Is it right to pay taxes to Caesar or not?' But Jesus, knowing their evil intent, said, 'You hypocrites, why are you trying to trap me? Show me the coin used for paying the tax.' They brought him a denarius, and he asked them, 'Whose portrait is this? And whose inscription?' 'Caesar's,' they replied. Then he said to them, 'Give to Caesar what is Caesar's, and to God what is God's.' When they heard this, they were amazed. So they left him and went away" (Matt. 22:17–22).

For teaching to be caught more than taught, using different techniques with modeling depends on incarnating your life with those you lead (see Section Two). Jesus spent three and a half years equipping the twelve apostles, focusing a lot of His attention on a few of them who would lead the others. But He didn't just focus on the Twelve. Sometimes He spoke to large crowds, other times to small groups, and for some others He gave individual attention. All His teachings, though, were appropriate to the situation and focused on His perfect modeling of the behavior of God. Jesus told a doubtful Philip, "Don't you know me, Philip, even after I have been among you such a long time? Anyone who has seen me has seen the Father" (John 14:9).

Though this kind of modeling/teaching lifestyle keeps the leader under the microscope, it positively becomes another impetus for holy living. It should be repeated as well that the modeling of godly behavior followed by explanatory teaching is valid only when leaders clearly understand that they're not trying *me-ism* to create their own disciples. We're making disciples for Christ, so we ought to be like the apostle Paul, who said, "Follow my example, as I follow the example of Christ" (1 Cor. 11:1).

Second, we often need to accompany our followers when they plan to take on a new task or ministry (Luke 9:12–17). Several years ago I planned to visit a sick parishioner in the hospital, and one of our newest church staff members asked to accompany me. Though he'd been in ministry awhile, he humbly admitted that he'd done little visitation. I agreed that he could come along, but he couldn't just observe—he'd need to participate as well. Because I was at his side, he had the confidence to move forward. At least if he didn't do well, I was there to encourage him. The wise King Solomon said, "Two are better than one, because they have a good return for their work: If one falls down, his friend can help him up. But pity the man who falls and has no one to help him up!" (Eccl. 4:9–10).

Third, when we are comfortable that those we are equipping are ready to go out on their own, we should send them on trial runs. In the church and in society, these trial runs are sometimes called "internships." They allow students to gain critical experience and confidence while still under the guidance of qualified supervisors.

Jesus used similar trial runs when He sent out seventy-two of His disciples two by two to minister in different towns. He gave them specific instructions and goals—preach the gospel, heal the sick, and cast out demons. He also told them to depend not on their own authority and power but on the authority and power He'd given them (Luke 10:1–23).

When the seventy-two returned from their short-term mission, Jesus did something many leaders of for-profit and nonprofit organizations fail to do: He debriefed them on their activities. When the disciples' returned, they joyfully celebrated their success, and Jesus celebrated with them, explaining what had been accomplished beyond their initial understanding. He warned them not to miss the main point of simply being a faithful follower of God. He said it was far more important to know that God loved them and to have received salvation than to exercise the power and authority Jesus had given them (Luke 10:20).

In the army one of the best practices adopted from the business world is the After Action Review (AAR). The AAR concept is simple: restate the goal of the activity or event, ask if the goal was accomplished, list a few things that were done well, and list several things that could be improved the next time the event or activity will be conducted. This simple debriefing technique enhances every organization and empowers people to achieve greater success.

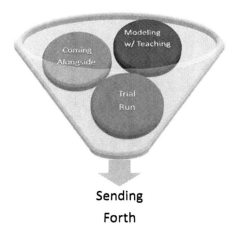

**Sending
Forth**

Finally, we see the concept of sending forth those we've trained and equipped. No one can remain a student forever. The Great Commandment leader always works to commission others to become loving servant leaders in their own right. Like parents whose goal is to raise their children to be spiritually and emotionally mature, productive adults, leaders function to equip others so they can be released into the world to accomplish their unique missions. Jesus said, "A student is not above his teacher, nor a servant above his master. It is enough for the student to be like his teacher, and the servant like his master" (Matt. 10:24–25). The apostle Luke records Jesus as saying, "A student is not above his teacher, but everyone who is fully trained will be like his teacher" (Luke 6:40). Therefore, every leader should help his or her "students" to become equippers.

All four authors of the Gospels record Jesus's commissioning of believers to go into the world to teach others the good news of salvation in Christ (Matt. 28:18; Mark 16:15; John 20:21; Acts 1:8). (See Chapter 13 for more about the Great Commission.)

LIFELONG LEARNING

Finally, the task of teaching and equipping others may seem overwhelming to many young leaders. But remember, the love of Christ motivates us, the power of His Spirit strengthens us, and the wisdom of God instructs us. "For who has known the mind of the Lord that he may instruct him? But we have the mind of Christ" (1 Cor. 2:16).

Though Great Commandment leaders continually depend on God for their strength, they also do everything within their power to gain wisdom and knowledge. "Wisdom is supreme; therefore get wisdom. Though it cost all you have, get understanding" (Prov. 4:7). They aren't going to rest until they learn all God has for them to learn. Being and becoming a Great Commandment leader is a lifelong learning process.

One encouraging way God helps those called to lead is the promise that He will instruct and teach us supernaturally through His Holy Spirit. Jesus told us that "the Counselor, the Holy Spirit, whom the Father will send in my name, will teach you all things and will remind you of everything I have said to you" (John 14:26). God Himself will teach the humble person willing to learn from Him.

Though John wrote the above verse primarily to the apostles, the principle applies to us today. The writer to the Hebrews reiterates the fact that God supernaturally equips His people. "May the God of peace, who through the blood of the eternal covenant brought back from the dead our Lord Jesus, that great Shepherd of the sheep, equip you with everything good for doing his will, and may he work in us what is pleasing to him, through Jesus Christ, to whom be glory for ever and ever.

Amen" (Heb. 13:20–21). God continues to equip His chosen leaders and bring them to completion.

Chapter Review Questions

1. What is the Great Commandment leader's primary work?
2. Describe the Great Commandment leader's three key equipping areas.
3. Why is "truth telling" so important to Great Commandment leadership?
4. The author writes, "Since the leader's character is critical to building trust, righteousness is a prerequisite for being a good leader." How do you respond to this statement?
5. What is the difference between preparing and equipping? Why is this distinction significant in better understanding Great Commandment leadership?
6. Describe the four methods of Jesus's pedagogy? What lessons might we learn from Jesus's teaching methods?

Chapter 9

Coaching Paradigm

CHRISTIAN COACHING

ONE OF THE most effective ways the Great Commandment leader can equip individuals and even small groups of disciples is through a biblically informed and Spirit-filled process called "coaching." Now, when you think about coaching, you may initially think of a football or basketball coach. If you're older, you might think of a coach as a bus or type of seat on an airplane. Though both descriptions of a coach may paint the picture of a person or thing that helps someone get to where he or she needs to go, the Christian idea of coaching may be defined as an intentional, transformational relationship focused on assisting someone to discover and accomplish what God has called him or her to do.

Coaching is not a fad. It has been around for millennia, and many excellent leaders continue to articulate and refine it. Ultimately, Christian coaching is about assisting and empowering others to achieve their God-given mission in life. I learned my coaching craft from several godly trainers, who used Bob Logan's book, *Coaching 101*, as the basis for their teachings. But for the purposes of this book, I've developed a simpler process one can effectively implement right away. I do, however, recommend that you attend a coaching clinic or training or that you read one of the many excellent books on coaching currently available (preferably one written by a Christian author).

BIBLICAL FOUNDATIONS

As I said before, the concept of coaching has been around for a long time. The apostle Paul alluded to coaching when he was "encouraging, comforting, and urging" the members of the church at Thessalonica (1 Thess. 2:11–12). These three words form a good description of someone who comes alongside others to assist them in achieving God's purposes. When the apostle Paul says he encouraged the Thessalonians, the Greek word *parakaleo* literally means one who is called alongside another. The verb form incorporates many different but analogous meanings including "to comfort, counsel, encourage, urge, appeal, or exhort."

In fact, *parakaleo* is the verb form of one of the names Jesus used to describe the Holy Spirit (John 14:26). Jesus says God will send the *Paraklētos* (translated "Counselor, Comforter, or Advocate") to indwell each believer and lead them into the truth (John 14:27). God, the Holy Spirit, is the ultimate coach!

Coaches comes alongside and encourage those being coached, "You can do this!" They comfort by reminding them that "with God's help you will be able to succeed, even in the face of difficulty." And they urge by exhorting, "You must accomplish what God has called you to do!"

One of the best scriptural examples of someone who was an effective coach is Barnabas, whose name means "son of encouragement." At great personal risk to his own reputation, Barnabas defended the apostle Paul when the church still despised and feared Paul (Acts 9:27). Barnabas provided needed resources to the church (Acts 4:37) and taught alongside Paul for several years (Acts 13:42–43), encouraging him every step of the way. Few Bible characters are depicted without serious character flaws, and one of them is Barnabas. He possessed both a righteous character and a clear vision to expand God's kingdom on earth. He was an excellent example of the Great Commandment leader.

When we become equippers of others, transforming them into God's servant leaders, we should become coaches who empower, encourage, and exhort those we lead. We come alongside, living a transparent life with our followers, leading by example, and sharing our love, wisdom, and resources with them.

Differences from Other Forms of Equipping

Because the word *parakaleo* can have diverse meanings, we should differentiate coaching from some other forms of equipping, specifically counseling, mentoring, and consulting. At the beginning of this discussion, I should clearly point out that transformational coaches don't tell those they coach what to do; instead they help them discover God's purposes for their lives. Because the Holy Spirit is the ultimate teacher/coach and Christ's messenger of the truth, the coach facilitates the discovery of what the Holy Spirit is saying to the person being coached.

First, what is unique about the coaching process is that the coach is primarily concerned with helping the "coachee" discover and achieve the particular goal God has called him or her to accomplish. Though done in a loving way, the coach primarily focuses the process on goal or task accomplishment.

Second, the coaching process doesn't involve a long-term, lifelong relationship like that of a mentor. The coaching relationship lasts from six months to a year. Because coaching is project or performance oriented, establishing a long-term relationship is unnecessary. The coach, however, may form a long-term discipleship relationship with those he or she coaches, but the coaching process must remain specifically task or project oriented. While the coach develops, exhorts, corrects, and even comforts the coachee, the goal is to ensure that the person being coached completes the project or goal for which God has called him or her.

task oriented

Lastly and most importantly, the coach never provides the solution to a problem or challenge the coachee attempts to solve. Mentors, counselors, and consultants often give solutions and options; they are sometimes even required to give an answer for a particular problem or challenge an individual or organization faces. Conversely, through asking probing questions, the Christian coach allows the Holy Spirit to be the true teacher and equipper of the person being coached.

don't solve coachee problems but ...

Again, in equipping and transforming others, the Great Commandment leader's primary focus is lovingly helping others achieve their God-given purpose. The table below may be helpful in differentiating between the various helping vocations.

Table 3: Differences between Helping Vocations

	Mentor	Counselor	Consultant	Coach
Focus	Personhood	Emotions	Performance	Project or task achievement
Process	Develops and disciple	Gains understanding	Changes implementation	Task and plan discovery
Guidance	Shares experiences	Provides good advice	Gives solutions and changes plan	Asks questions to evoke a response

Continued

	Mentor	Counselor	Consultant	Coach
Time Frame	Long term	Medium term	Short term	Short to medium term
Style	Informal	Professional-formal	Professional-formal	Friendly but task oriented
Goal	Personal development	Healing and recovery	Correcting problems	Project/task completion
Relationship	Volunteer	Paid	Paid	Paid or Volunteer

COACHING PROCESS: THE FOUR DS

The coaching process can be described as four distinct stages we can remember as The Four Ds: (1) discover the dream, (2) digging deeper, (3) develop the plan, and (4) debrief until complete. The first stage is designed to help the coachee discover the dream or, in other words, articulate what God is asking him or her to accomplish. The apostle James says, "If any of you

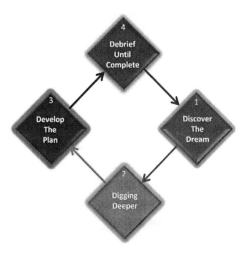

lacks wisdom, he should ask God, who gives generously to all" (James 1:5). Scripture also calls on the godly to seek counsel (Prov. 15:22). Discovering what God wants someone else to do may be the most difficult part of the coaching process. It might be helpful for the coach to see a resume or get some good background information from the coachee prior to the first appointment.

Coachees sometimes have very broad objectives. Here are few I've heard: "to become more spiritual," "to grow my church or ministry," or "to fix my ministry or organization." The purpose of the discover-the-dream stage, however, is to articulate one or two specific, measurable, and attainable goals one can work on over six months to a year. Working on one or two specific challenges normally increases the overall effectiveness of any organization or ministry. Therefore, the coach should be clear with the coachee and not make grandiose promises. The coach should help the coachee clearly articulate what he or she believes God is calling him or her to do one step at a time.

One recent example of the discover-the-dream stage was my involvement in helping a pastor decide whether to develop an elder board (leadership team) for his newly formed church. Once he decided the time was right to do so, we moved to the next stage. The discover-the-dream stage should take only one or two meetings. If the intent of the coaching process is to discover "life goals" rather than a specific project or task, however, this stage may last longer.

In the second stage, the digging-deeper phase of the coaching relationship, the coach asks the coachee to orally discuss potential courses of actions, challenges, and resource issues that may either help or hinder him or her to accomplish the goal. Unlike a consultant, who should be an expert in the area of assistance, the coach doesn't need specific experience with the task the person being coached is trying to accomplish. The coach's function is only to ask penetrating questions to encourage the coachee to think in different ways about the task. Sometimes having little experience with a task or project may even be better for the coach. If coaches have too much experience with someone else's issue, they may be tempted to give the coachee the other person's solution.

In the digging-deeper stage, the coachee conducts an individual brainstorming session while the coach challenges him or her to think creatively "outside the box." If the coachee gets stuck, the coach may ask specific questions, such as, "Have you thought about what other people may have done to get the resources they needed for a similar project?" Here is where you may assign homework to the person being coached. Ask the coachee to do research and report during the next meeting. Mentors share their experiences in dealing with an issue, counselors might suggest a book they found helpful, and consultants will often do the research for the client. But coaches know that the person they are trying to equip needs to learn how to take ownership of what God is calling him or her to do. That is why the coach functions as a prodder or coaxer rather than someone who provides advice. Jesus was a master at this technique, often asking the hard question, "What do you think?" (Matt. 17:25; 18:12; 21:28).

The third stage is develop-the-plan stage. Once coachees have articulated their measurable goals and understand some activities that will help them accomplish their tasks, they will need to develop specific actions for which they can be held accountable. Some coaches may have their clients working on multiple action steps at the same time, but it may be advisable to start with just one or two action steps that will be easy to accomplish.

There's a strategy for this. Achieving some initial success will encourage the person being coached. If you try to tackle the most difficult parts of the plan first, coachees might become discouraged if things don't work out and want to give up. Don't get bogged down in this stage. It should take only one to two sessions to develop a preliminary action plan. Of course, while working toward the final stage, the plan will probably need to be adjusted.

The fourth D is the debrief-until-complete stage. This longest phase is designed to continually assess the quality of decisions and action steps taken between each meeting. During this phase coachees are held accountable to the plan they developed. This process continues until the project or goal is completed. The debriefings should follow a particular format listed in the coaching appointment section below.

coachee accountable for plan developed until project completed

Just because coachees achieve the desired goal or complete the project successfully doesn't necessarily mean the relationship with the coach must come to an end. The whole process can restart with a different goal or task the person being coached believes is important. The decision must be mutual, of course, and both parties should feel free to end the coaching relationship anytime during the process.

mentor-like?

Coaching Appointment—C.A.R.E.

A good coaching appointment format is critical to the success of the coaching process. Normally, a coaching appointment lasts one hour and occurs only once a month. Coaches can offer an additional appointment between regularly scheduled ones if a critical question or action step is unresolved.

meeting guidelines

1 hour
1 per month

I have boiled down the coaching appointment to four easy-to-remember steps: celebrate success, assess the challenges, focus on resource needs, and engage next steps. The acronym C.A.R.E. is so named to remind Great Commandment leaders that they first and foremost share the love of God with those they lead.

The first part of the appointment, called "celebrate success," focuses on the relationship to correspond with the biblical injunction to be encouragers (1 Thess. 5:11). Whatever went

note whatever went well

well since the previous appointment is cause for celebrating and giving praise and thanks to God. One principle of effective leadership is to discover what others do well, celebrate it, and have them do more of it. Though only a small amount of the hour is dedicated to this part, it is critical in building the confidence of the coachee.

C.A.R.E. Coaching Appointment

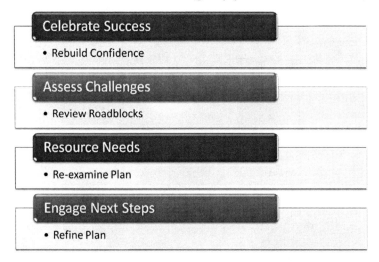

Celebrate Success
- Rebuild Confidence

Assess Challenges
- Review Roadblocks

Resource Needs
- Re-examine Plan

Engage Next Steps
- Refine Plan

The second part of the appointment is devoted to assess the *discuss/assess challenges?* challenges that occurred when the coachee tried to implement the plan. During initial meetings, roadblocks to success can be discussed. If they continue to plague the project, the coach and the coachee should spend more time considering alternative *alternatives?* strategies to overcome these barriers.

Reviewing the impediments to success naturally leads to the third part of the meeting, which focuses on resource needs. *resources needed* Resources refer not only to money and people but also to information, assessment tools, technology, and so on. This is *coach can help –* where the coach's prior experience and influence as a leader come *i.e., like a mentor??*

into play. He or she can point the coachee in the right place or direction to ensure that he or she has the best opportunity to succeed. One of the best tools I've used in coaching is a simple time-use analysis. Many leaders face difficulties because they're ineffective or inefficient at managing time, their most precious resource. In addition, the coach might even suggest books, articles, websites, or people who can assist the coachee.

time mgmt !

The last part of the coaching appointment is to engage next steps, refine the plan, and establish new action steps to be taken during the coming month. The coach takes the opportunity to articulate the lessons learned from the month before. He or she asks the coachee to apply them to future planning so the same mistakes aren't made and the previous roadblocks avoided. Discerning God's plan is a process that takes time. The process of discerning God's specific desire for the coachee's project may not be instantaneous.

what next ?

Finally and most importantly, the appointment should start with prayer and—I strongly believe—end in prayer. We seek the Holy Spirit's guidance and wisdom, not our own ingenuity. Ultimately, we want to do God's will, not our own (Matt. 6:10; Luke 24:22). Prayer that admits our needs and seeks God's guidance goes a long way to discerning the plan God wants for the life and vocation of the coachee.

Begin/End with prayer !

CRITICAL COACHING COMPETENCIES

Good coaches will possess and develop several areas of competence. Of course, they need to possess a deep, personal relationship with Christ. Discernment, patience, clear communication, and a good understanding of strategic vision (see Chapter 11) are just a few of the skills an effective coach should possess.

By far the most critical coaching competency is the ability to ask timely, thought-provoking questions. Jesus was a master at asking deep, penetrating questions to help His disciples and

asking questions

others gain understanding. Open-ended questions, those that do not seek a yes or no answer, always help the coachee to think critically and answer more comprehensively. Also, asking "why" questions helps the coach and coachee better understand the coachee's motivation. I could list a series of good questions to ask in the coaching session, but you can find hundreds of excellent coaching questions simply by searching the World Wide Web for "coaching questions."

Using scaling questions is one of the most effective ways to understand the importance of a particular course of action or even a motivation. For instance, a scaling question might ask, "On a scale of one to ten, how committed are you to that course of action?" The scaling question can be used in many different situations. It gives clarity not only to the person being coached but also to the coach.

Interestingly, though the ability to ask good questions is the most critical coaching skill, one needs a prerequisite skill just to formulate a good question. That skill is listening. Coaches should refrain from commenting too often and continually ask themselves, "Why am I talking?" (W.A.I.T.). Another good listening technique is to restate what the coachee said (feedback) so he or she knows that the coach clearly understands the situation. Feedback questions also help keep the coaching conversation focused.

For many seasoned leaders, listening may be the most difficult part of coaching. Potential coachees may choose their coach based on his or her experience or reputation. Coachees often challenge the coach, simply seeking good advice. The good coach listens intently not only to words but also to the coachee's body language and vocal tone. Listening helps the coach ask deep, penetrating questions that help the coachee hear the Holy Spirit speaking to him or her. Christian coaches should be wary of putting on their pastor or consultant hats unless they see some destructive behavior about to occur.

CHALLENGES TO EFFECTIVE COACHING

The most significant pitfalls to effective coaching are not listening, talking too much, and giving advice; but there are others we should be aware of. Here are a few problems to avoid in the coaching relationship: (1) not giving undivided attention to the coachee (this is especially dangerous during coaching over the phone), (2) letting the coachee push your buttons, (3) solving the coachee's problems, (4) getting frustrated by the coachee's lack of clarity, (5) asking patronizing leading questions, and (6) getting caught up in the coachee's drama. Remember, being a coach and a Great Commandment leader isn't about you; it's about the person being coached.

In the many coaching sessions I've conducted with pastors, ministry leaders, and others, the most amazing thing I've encountered is how often coachees quickly discover the answers to their own problems, issues, or challenges. For one pastor I coached, it was uncanny how many times he realized he had the answer when I was about to ask a question. I wasn't surprised when his church tripled in size during the six months after we began our coaching relationship.

Coaching done well is by far the most effective tool in equipping others to be successful in their vocations and ministries.

Chapter Review Questions

1. What is coaching? What's unique about the Christian coaching process?
2. Why is Barnabas viewed as an ideal model for coaching? What coaching lessons might we learn from Barnabas?
3. The author presents a table distinguishing a coach from a mentor, counselor, and consultant. What are the differences among the four vocations?

4. Describe the four stages of the coaching process. What are your thoughts about them?
5. Describe the four steps of the coaching appointment C.A.R.E. process. What are your thoughts about them?
6. What are some of the competencies a good coach should obtain? How might you nurture these competencies?
7. What are some pitfalls to good coaching? What might you do to help address those issues?

Chapter 10

Multiplication Paradigm

PARADIGM SHIFTS

THOMAS KUHN COINED the term "paradigm shift" in his book *The Structure of Scientific Revolutions*. Kuhn's thesis was that major scientific discoveries weren't the product of the steady accumulation of researched information but of the innovative and sudden introduction of radically new ideas. These amazing discoveries changed the way people thought about long-held beliefs and forced the scientific community to give up on previously agreed-upon theories. Today, the notion of paradigm shifts has been applied to almost every area of life.

In Chapter 8 we introduced the idea of an equipping paradigm. This paradigm shift moved us away from the minister-centric model common in most established churches and ministries in the West. It led us to a new model (disciple centric), where equipping disciples to do the ministry becomes the norm (1 Peter 2:9). In the equipping paradigm the leader doesn't focus on doing the ministry himself, but training those who will. Most pastors and ministry leaders agree with this biblical axiom, but few actually practice it. Remember, equipping others so they can do ministry is the Great Commandment leader's primary function (Eph. 4:11–12).

In Chapter 9 we introduced the coaching paradigm, shifting the common understanding of equipping as "information exchange" to one that expects the person being coached to discern, investigate, and create a solution for their own ministry tasks and goals. The coaching paradigm shift moves the leader away from the role of expert to one of facilitator, helping others to discover what the Holy Spirit, the true expert, has to teach the follower of Christ.

Interestingly, Thomas Kuhn didn't discover the notion of paradigm shifts; he just articulated it in a new way. Over two thousand years ago, Jesus referred to them when He said we should not "pour new wine into old wineskins. If [you] do, the skins will burst, the wine will run out and the wineskins will be ruined. No, [you should] pour new wine into new wineskins, and both are preserved" (Matt. 9:17). Jesus instructed us not to put His new, radical ideas into our old paradigms (wineskins). Remember when He said, "A new command I give you: Love one another. As I have loved you, so you must love one another" (John 13:34). Jesus wanted us to see loving each other in a new, radical, and self-sacrificing way. It requires us to renew our minds or shift our paradigms and not be conformed to the way the world would shape us (Rom. 12:2).

MULTIPLICATION, NOT GROWTH

The multiplication paradigm shifts our thinking from growing the size of a ministry or an organization to equipping a small group of leaders who can multiply others and grow their ministries as well. When Jesus told the apostles to "go and make disciples of all nations" (Matt. 28:19), He didn't commission them to do so by themselves. Jesus sent the apostles primarily to train others around the world, then leave qualified servant leaders in each town where they'd establish a local church (Titus 1:5). The process of multiplication focuses on replicating disciples, not accumulating them. Great Commandment leaders don't exist to create followers but to replicate their leadership DNA in their followers.

Unfortunately, many of the largest ministries in the United States became large not through multiplication but by attracting followers away from ministries that couldn't provide the same quality or number of services or programs. These megaministries are often heralded and their leaders lauded, but the net result for the church has been fewer disciples, not more. We should note that since the megachurch movement began, overall church attendance has sharply declined.

Conversely, the church has historically experienced its greatest growth when individual leaders and ministries have multiplied. This fact is evident today in China, Africa, and South America, where disciples and churches are growing at a rapid rate—not because of megachurches or charismatic leaders but because of multiplied individuals and ministries.

MULTIPLYING INDIVIDUALS OR GROUPS

Instead of spending all His time with the multitudes, Jesus poured His life into only twelve of His followers. He spent most of His time with only a few: Peter, James, and John. Multiplication of a few is the secret of true kingdom growth. The concept may seem paradoxical. How can less equal more? Maybe it does in the same way that the last shall be first (Mark 10:31)—or in the fact that when we lose our lives, we will find them (Matt 10:39)—or in how the humble will be exalted (Luke 18:14).

Jesus knew He had only a short time to prepare His future servant leaders. Therefore, without neglecting the masses,

He focused on equipping His twelve disciples so they could multiply others. This focus on training a few may be the toughest paradigm to shift. Our culture has so well indoctrinated us into a growth paradigm. In his book *Hurtling Toward Oblivion*, Richard Swenson makes the case that the world is trapped in a destructive cycle of wanting more. Swenson calls humanity's insatiable desire for more "profusion" and says it will ultimately destroy us.

Unfortunately, too many leaders of large ministries cannot make the multiplication shift because they've allocated most of their resources—time, people, and money—to growing their ministries. By focusing the majority of resources on the main weekly gathering or the big outreach event, most large ministries are ineffective in equipping small groups of individuals who can then multiply others.

The author of Hebrews warned about this problem in the early church, when he noted that believers were acting more like consumers than producers (or reproducers). "Though by this time you ought to be teachers, you need someone to teach you the elementary truths of God's Word all over again" (Heb. 5:12). Even then many followers were being trained not to lead but to follow in a codependent manner.

The key Bible verse that helped me make the multiplication shift was 2 Timothy 2:2. "And the things you have heard me say in the presence of many witnesses entrust to reliable men who will also be qualified to teach others." This verse became the basis and motto of The Center for Leader Multiplication, the ministry I started to equip ministry leaders. With those words the apostle Paul reminded young Timothy to spend more time multiplying leaders who would then multiply others. The apostle Paul wanted to ensure that Timothy understood he wasn't only called and appointed to teach others, but was also gifted and anointed to equip and multiply others to teach others.

In one church I pastored, several of the more "mature" members said I focused too much on evangelism and outreach; they encouraged me to lead more Bible studies. I lovingly told them that they didn't need more Bible studies; they needed to obey what they'd learned and start making disciples themselves. The apostle Paul challenged one of his best students to "do the work of the evangelist, discharge all the duties of your ministry" (2 Tim. 4:5). As he approached the end of his life and ministry, Paul wanted to ensure that Timothy would continue the work of multiplication.

The multiplication paradigm is intrinsically designed to bear more fruit than a growth paradigm. Tom Etema of EQUIP Ministries brought this point to light when he said, "If you had an event where 100 souls a day for 30 years were converted, a total of 11 million people would be reached. However, if you reached 1 soul a year and taught them to reach one soul a year and then each one subsequently discipled 1 soul a year, this process would yield 9 billion souls reached in 30 years!"[11] The table below provides a clear, visual representation of what it would be like if one disciple trained one other disciple for one year, followed by each disciple subsequently training one new disciple each year.

Table 4: Multiplying Disciples Exponentially

Year	Number Discipled and Trained
1	2
2	4
4	16
6	64
8	256
10	1,024

Continued

Year	Number Discipled and Trained
12	4,096
14	16,384
20	1,048,576
30	8,589,934,592

Of course, the multiplication paradigm must be in the DNA, if you will, of those leading the ministry. Great Commandment leaders must abandon the old growth theory, stop focusing on how they might change the world, and concentrate their efforts on equipping a band of followers, who will become self-replicating disciple makers.

I heard an amusing story of a young convert who was zealous about sharing the message of salvation in Jesus Christ. He told his pastor about his idea to change the world. He planned to solicit the richest Christians around the globe so on one day in the near future every single person on earth would hear the gospel. All he needed to do was raise enough money so every television, radio, and computer would deliver the message of the gospel at one hour on one particular day.

He reminded his pastor of Matthew 24:14. "And this gospel of the kingdom will be preached in the whole world as a testimony to all nations, and then the end will come." If they could just present the gospel to every person on earth at once, he reasoned, Jesus would return.

The gracious pastor said, "That's a great idea, and I appreciate your zeal for the Lord. By the way, I know you've got a wife and three children. Have you shared the gospel with them yet?" The enthusiastic new believer lowered his head in shame and acknowledged that he hadn't. The pastor said, "Maybe after you've shared Jesus with your family and your neighbors, we can move on to the rest of the world."

For the individual believer the multiplication process starts in the home. Each parent is a servant leader to his or her children. If parents successfully disciple their children, those children will possess the multiplication code in their spiritual DNA. Unfortunately, goods and services-driven ministries in the United States have fostered a consumerist attitude among Christians. Many American Christians have been conditioned to expect the local church to take the responsibility to disciple their children. This responsibility, however, belongs to their parents and family; the responsibility of the local church leadership is to equip parents to do so. If we can't use the multiplication paradigm in our own homes and personal lives, we'll be unable to implement it on a larger scale.

MULTIPLYING MINISTRIES OR ORGANIZATIONS

At the time of the apostles, the churches were small. For one thing, due to persecution, the first Christians met secretly in their homes. But even as they experienced more freedom to gather, the original churches grew by multiplication (or division), not by adding more space to accommodate more people. When a group of disciples outgrew their space, they simply appointed the most equipped believer to start a new church. Therefore, the ancient church grew by multiplication.

One unique way the original apostles multiplied the church wasn't by inviting new converts into their personal homes but by meeting in the homes of the newest disciples. "When [Lydia] and the members of her household were baptized, she invited us to her home. 'If you consider me a believer in the Lord,' she said, 'come and stay at my house'" (Acts 16:15). Holding meetings in new believers' houses created a sense that newly trained believers would need to continue the ministry long after the apostles left their homes.

In business vernacular we might best understand the concept of multiplication as franchising. McDonalds® didn't grow big by building bigger restaurants to accommodate more customers; no, those in charge simply built a new restaurant where most of their new customers lived. When Great Commandment leaders focus on multiplying leaders, who then multiply other leaders, they shouldn't be discouraged by the initial small number of converts. They can refer back to the exponential multiplication table and redouble their efforts to equip a select few who will continue the pattern of multiplication. Therefore, if leaders started a ministry or organization, their goal to multiply leaders who could multiply that ministry or organization at another location would have a greater impact than if they had grown the ministry larger with the focus on their leader.

One of the main tenets of The Center for Leader Multiplication is to equip small numbers of ministry leaders by giving them tools they can use to train others. Several times per year, I lead seminars for about twenty-five ministry leaders. At the end of the seminar, participants receive training material, a CD of the original materials in an editable format (so they can manipulate them), and a covenant for participants to sign, ensuring that they will use the materials to train others in their ministries or organizations. We give all this to participants free of charge, motivated by Matthew 10:8. "Freely you have received, freely give."

As a Great Commandment leader, your desire to multiply your ministry or organization should lead you to recruit people who have unique ideas for their own ministries. Then coach and equip them to succeed. Having multiplication as part of your organization's DNA will help your ministry to launch new ministries or organizations that will also multiply. At Crestmont Alliance Church (CAC), where I served as lead minister, I'm privileged to say that at least five new ministries are successfully operating today because of the emphasis the leadership at CAC put on equipping and multiplying people and ministries. Instead of inviting those disciples to help me grow the church, I assisted them to fulfill God's call on their lives and multiply their ministries.

MULTIPLYING COMMUNITIES

Finally, as multiplication DNA becomes ingrained in the lifestyles of those you lead, individuals and ministries will multiply, as will the impact they have on surrounding communities. The prophet Ezekiel described God's desire to multiply not only the people of Israel and their ministries but also their communities. "I am concerned for you and will look on you with favor; you will be plowed and sown, and I will multiply the number of people upon you, even the whole house of Israel. The towns will be inhabited and the ruins rebuilt. I will multiply the number of men and animals upon you, and they will be fruitful and become numerous. I will settle people on you as in the past and will make you prosper more than before. Then you will know that I am the Lord" (Ezek. 36:9–11).

In the multiplication strategy Jesus had in mind, He envisioned just a few disciples having a major impact in changing whole communities. Jesus said that His kingdom would start small like a mustard seed. "Yet when planted, it grows and becomes the largest of all garden plants, with such big branches that the birds of the air can perch in its shade" (Mark 4:32). Again, Jesus said His kingdom was like a small amount of "yeast that a woman took and mixed into a large amount of flour until it worked all through the dough" (Matt. 13:33).

That is not to say that Great Commandment leaders aren't concerned about growth. Growth is important, but to grow a ministry or organization the way God wants it to grow becomes more important than the growth itself. No Christian leaders should look back at any success they might have enjoyed in ministry and attribute it to their skills, ingenuity, or charisma. Like the apostle Paul, they should say, "I planted the seed and another watered it, but God made it grow" (1 Cor. 3:6, author's paraphrase).

Chapter Review Questions

1. The author addresses the concept of "paradigm shifts." How have the insights of Great Commandment leaders shifted your leadership paradigm presuppositions?
2. What is the difference between "multiplication" and "growth?" Why is this difference significant in better understanding the multiplication paradigm?
3. The author writes, "Great Commandment leaders don't exist to create followers but to replicate their leadership DNA in their followers." How do you respond to this statement?
4. In the multiplication paradigm, why is focusing on fewer people considered more effective than focusing on more people?
5. What lessons might we learn from the early church regarding multiplying churches?

Chapter 11

Outcome Paradigm

Vision, Planning, and Execution

A RESPECTED ADMINISTRATOR at Nyack College once confided to me that many came to him with ideas for improving his department, but few were willing to help. "The world is filled with people with great ideas," he said, "but very few who are capable of executing them successfully."

In the Introduction, I mentioned that the key distinguishing difference between a leader and a follower is vision. A good leader envisions what can or ought to be, devises a plan to accomplish the vision, and then successfully executes that plan. To be a Great Commandment leader, you must articulate and execute a vision for the positive, transformational change of individuals, organizations, and even entire communities.

Unfortunately, I'm surprised by how few Christian ministry leaders have neither the ability nor the desire to cast a Spirit-inspired vision to affect positive change for their people, their ministries, or their communities. Many in positions of authority have discovered all sorts of ways to avoid this difficult but critical

helpers needed

A good leader

most don't

aspect of leadership. Some leaders claim they don't know how to cast vision, and others have tried to execute a vision plan that failed. The most common form of vision avoidance is pointing to the perception that we're not in control of the future—that only God has power over the future. According to extreme determinists, God is completely sovereign, so we shouldn't presume to think we can understand or influence the future. This fatalistic worldview is inconsistent with Christian theology (Josh. 24:2; Matt. 5:39; Gal. 5:1; 2 Cor. 3:17).

While serving in Iraq, I encountered many uneducated citizens. As we tried to help them make positive change, they replied to what we said with "*Insha' Allah!*" The Arabic term, when translated into English, means, "If God wills it, it will happen." This defeatist point of view says that only God can actually cause change in the world; humans are powerless. To many of the Iraqis I met, freewill is a dangerous fantasy Westerners invented.

But fatalism isn't the worldview of only many Islam proponents. Some seemingly pious Christians erroneously use the term "God willing" in a fatalistic way, too. They use the words as an escape clause should their plans go awry. The French phrase *c'est la vie*, which means "such is life," also promotes a fatalistic attitude. In addition, the famous song "*Que Sera, Sera*" (Whatever Will Be, Will Be) is yet another example of Western acceptance of philosophical fatalism. Furthermore, our culture's pursuit of postmodernism, with its rejection of objective truth, will create an increasing acceptance of fatalism.

The Bible tells us that even though God is sovereign and ultimately in control of all things, He expects us to work for the good of all, "envisioning a preferable future" for His people and executing a Spirit-inspired plan to accomplish His will. In the book of Proverbs, we read that "a wise man thinks ahead; a fool doesn't, and even brags about it!" (13:16 LB). God wants us to plan and be wise about the future. "Do not those who plot evil go astray? But those who plan what is good find love and faithfulness" (Prov. 14:22). Making plans to do good requires God's wisdom and godly advice but doesn't usurp God's sovereignty or His authority (Prov. 16:3; 20:18; 21:5).

Though a well-known verse in Proverbs—"Where there is no vision, the people perish" (38:18 KJV)—pertains primarily to scriptural revelation, the word *vision* (Hebrew: *chazown*) refers to understanding God's dreams or vision for His people. The reality is that many ministries and organizations are stagnant or declining because they don't pursue a compelling, God-inspired vision. In addition, those who have vision fail to properly execute the plan to achieve it. Bishop Joseph Garlington aptly warned, "Where there is no plan, the vision will perish."

For Great Commandment leaders, having vision and making plans does not mean we are trying to alter God's future. We only direct our present activity to be in line with His perfect, loving will.

OUTCOME VISION FOR TRANSFORMING INDIVIDUALS

To envision "God's preferable future" and conduct planning require adopting an outcome paradigm. Instead of thinking sequentially, we first envision the end product. The paradigm shift needed to become outcome oriented means refraining from thinking about first steps before clearly understanding what success, the outcome, looks like. Then we work backward to devise our plan and work the plan, adjusting it along the way until completion. This process may sound very simple, but it requires that we are in tune with God and hearing from Him, not simply coming up with a random numerical goal or devising some clever scheme.

Remember, the function of Great Commandment leaders is ultimately to equip others to fulfill God's plan for their lives and ministries. Having that core mission as the basis for ministry makes envisioning the outcome a lot easier. Because God has given us the mission, discerning His vision shouldn't be too difficult. In fact, the apostle Paul told us about God's desired outcome for transforming individuals. "We proclaim [Christ], admonishing and teaching everyone with all wisdom, so that we may present everyone perfect in Christ. To this end I labor, struggling with all his energy, which so powerfully works in me" (Col. 1:28–29).

Paul (vision)

The apostle Paul labored with God's power to achieve a particular end by particular means. He wanted everyone he equipped to reach his or her full potential—to be perfect in Christ. He had a plan to accomplish this goal: (1) proclaim repentance in Jesus as Lord and Savior of all, (2) admonish or warn disciples against ungodly (or unloving) living, and (3) teach them to work toward fulfilling Christ's Great Commission in the spirit of the Great Commandment.

We know Paul sensed that he'd accomplished his proclamation work because he told the church at Rome, "It has always been my ambition to preach the gospel where Christ was not known.…But now…there is no more place for me to work in these regions" (Rom. 15:20, 23). He had a measurable methodology to understand when he finished his work in a particular region.

And when Paul completed his part of the work, he left multiplying leaders in every place so they could continue the work. His end product and ours is reproducing disciples. Before we move to a new place or take on a new assignment, we should ensure that those we worked with can carry on the work and replicate themselves. When we do not know what the end product looks like, we'll never feel as if we were successful or even accomplished anything of value. Making disciples who can make disciples—that is our desired outcome.

end product: reproducing disciples

Paul's three actions to achieve the outcome of replicating disciples correspond with the process shown in the table below.

The first step is to proclaim a change in the thinking of others about who God is and what He's like (see Chapter 1). Most people have wrong thinking about who Christ is (2 Cor. 5:16). *first function* Our first function is to help others know the love of God in Christ (change in mind or attitudes). Next, we exhort those *2nd* who have come to Christ to allow His love to transform their behavior (change in actions). Finally, we teach and equip them *3rd* to do the ministry of loving God, loving others, and multiplying God's love around the world (change in state). When we use this simple, outcome-oriented process, creating tools to measure individual progress shouldn't be difficult.

Table 5: Outcome Process for Transforming Individuals
(Adapted from the "Logic Model")

Initial Transformation: "Change of Mind/ Attitudes"	Intermediate Transformation: "Change in Actions"	Long-Term Transformation: "Change in State"
Understands God's love and salvation in Christ	Begins to engage in study of Scripture, prayer, and fellowship with Christians	Holy living is a priority of life; accept responsibility to be a servant leader.
No longer in opposition to God or His church	Begins to curb sinful activities	Is active in church and local community service
Makes a firm commitment to follow Christ	Begins to be equipped for ministry	Is actively involved in reproducing himself or herself
Understands position in Christ	Begins to take on leadership roles	Is actively involved in an equipping ministry (coaching)

OUTCOME VISION FOR TRANSFORMING GROUPS AND ORGANIZATIONS

Understanding the outcome paradigm may be easier when we apply it to organizations. Though it may be easier to understand in an organizational context, however, the execution of a plan to achieve it may be more difficult. Nevertheless, using a backward-planning strategy still applies in an organizational setting.

In the *Parable of The Tower Builder*, Jesus describes the difficult decision we all must make before choosing to become one of His disciples. He also gives us an excellent vision-planning tool. "Suppose one of you wants to build a tower. Will he not first sit down and estimate the cost to see if he has enough money to complete it? For if he lays the foundation and is not able to finish it, everyone who sees it will ridicule him, saying, 'This fellow began to build and was not able to finish'" (Luke 14:28–30).

Jesus begins with the desired outcome—"One of you wants to build a tower." He begins the visioning process with the end product in mind.

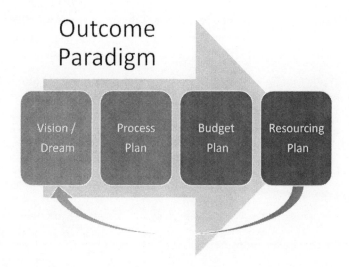

Outcome Paradigm

Vision / Dream — Process Plan — Budget Plan — Resourcing Plan

I introduced this outcome paradigm to the leadership at the last church I pastored. I instructed members of each department to produce and submit a budget each year, based not on the previous year's cash flow but on their vision for the upcoming year. They first needed to determine what God wanted them to "build." Before they were even allowed to think about resources, money, or anything related to a plan, they needed to dream God's dreams for their ministry. They needed to see the outcome first.

budget based on vision

Next Jesus asks, "Will he not first sit down?" Sitting down is the process of planning what nonfinancial resources (personnel, materials, time, and so on) you will need to build your "tower." The five Ws (who, what, when, where, and why) will help you chart what achieving your vision will take. Please note: at this stage of the planning process, do not be concerned about where you will get the needed personnel and resources. Just discern what nonfinancial resources you will need to achieve the end result.

plan of non-financial resources

5 Ws

don't worry about where resources will come from

The next step in outcome planning is determining how much the vision will cost. Again, at this stage of the process you determine not where the resources will come from but what the project or ministry will require financially. Too often as we plan, we miss the vision because we are overly concerned about the lack of resources. But when we truly understand God's vision, we rest assured that God will "meet all your needs according to his glorious riches in Christ Jesus" (Phil. 4:19). Hudson Taylor, the visionary missionary to China, said, "God's work done in God's way will never lack God's supply." We cannot allow our fears of failure to keep us from envisioning God-sized dreams for the advancement of His kingdom. But be aware that during the outcome-planning process, sometimes you or others will be tempted to move away from the vision or minimize it.

Then how much $ (don't worry about where $ will come from)

←

warning

In the final stage we will create a plan to secure the necessary resources to complete the project. Jesus said we ought "to see if [we have] enough money to complete it." In this last phase of

Finally, create a plan

*cash
flow
analysis,
looking
everywhere*

outcome planning, we complete a cash flow analysis, income or sales projection, recruiting, and/or fundraising planning. All avenues for securing needed resources must also be discussed and thoroughly examined before deciding on an adjustment to the vision or desired outcome. Nonetheless, starting a project that is severely short of resources, especially one envisioned to advance God's kingdom, may bring "ridicule" upon the leadership and the kingdom of God.

*never
stops!*

The outcome planning process can be used again when a project is completed successfully or when a yearly ministry and budget review is conducted, even when a new vision is necessary for a ministry or organization that is floundering. The practice of envisioning and revisioning should never end. It should always be done prayerfully, patiently, and continually. The Great Commandment leader always looks for new ways and dreams God-sized dreams to transform ministries and organizations for God's kingdom advancement.

OUTCOME VISION FOR TRANSFORMING COMMUNITIES

Great Commandment leaders—indeed, any Christian ministry—should never assume that transformational vision is limited to individuals or organizations. God wants to transform whole communities and expects His anointed leaders to possess the vision to accomplish His desires.

During the Jewish exile in Babylon, God's prophets told the Israelites about the vision God had for them. The prophecy was not only an encouragement to the people of a preferable future but also a picture of the work they needed to do to accomplish the vision. Isaiah prophesied that God's people would "rebuild the ancient ruins and…raise up the age-old foundations; you will be called Repairer of Broken Walls, Restorer of Streets with Dwellings" (Isa. 58:12). In community development work, the Great Commandment leader and all who work beside him or her should be known as community life "restorers" and "rebuilders."

[margin note: community life restorers or rebuilders]

While in exile, Nehemiah received a specific vision about the rebuilding of the wall in Jerusalem. He traveled into the city and, without telling anyone what he was doing, "set out during the night with a few men. I had not told anyone what my God had put in my heart to do for Jerusalem" (Neh. 2:12). As we begin to see a preferable future for our communities, we will move in faith and survey the needs, hearing from God what our role is and then painting a vision picture to encourage others to work alongside us. Once Nehemiah was satisfied that he understood what God had called him to do, he announced, "'Come, let us rebuild the wall of Jerusalem.'"…[And] they replied, 'Let us start rebuilding'" (Neh. 2:17–18). Nehemiah then created a sophisticated plan, which included all the people of the community in the process.

[margin note: painting a vision picture]

Like Nehemiah, God calls the Great Commandment leader to incarnate into a specific community and receive God's vision for that community. Seeing that picture of what a rebuilt community looks like (especially one at risk), communicating a Spirit-filled vision to the people, and working side by side with the residents of the community are all part of being a Great Commandment leader. Community transformation is a matter of love and justice.

Chapter Review Questions

1. Why is vision casting so important for Great Commandment leadership?
2. Why does the outcome paradigm require end-product thinking instead of sequential thinking?
3. Describe the three actions Paul used to achieve the outcome of replicating disciples?

4. The author presents an outcome process table for transforming individuals. What lessons might you learn regarding initial, intermediate, and lifelong transformation?
5. What Great Commandment lessons regarding vision and community building might we learn from Nehemiah?

Chapter 12

Justice Paradigm

LOVE AND JUSTICE

THE GREAT CIVIL rights leader and pastor, Rev. Martin
Luther King Jr., famously wrote from his jail cell in Birmingham,
Alabama, "Injustice anywhere is a threat to justice everywhere."
Sadly, ungodly men and women throughout the world seek
to oppress the weak, the impoverished, and the uneducated.
Yet God is intensely concerned about justice for all who are
oppressed or otherwise denied His blessings through the
actions of sinful humans. Because of their love for God and
their neighbors, Great Commandment leaders will be actively
involved in working for justice.

Though great philosophers have debated justice for
centuries, the definition is simple: treat people fairly and
impartially. The writer of Proverbs echoed this simple
understanding of justice when he stated that "evil men do not
understand justice, but those who seek the Lord understand
it fully" (Prov. 28:5). In Scripture justice focuses primarily on
those oppressed or being treated unfairly by those in power.

"justice" defined

People who work for justice "speak up for those who cannot speak for themselves, for the rights of all who are destitute. [They] speak up and judge fairly; defend the rights of the poor and needy" (Prov. 31:8–9).

The desire for justice is intrinsically tied to God's love for His creation. Love and justice, the Word tells us, go hand in hand. The psalmist declared that the "Lord loves righteousness and justice; the earth is full of his unfailing love" (Ps. 33:5). Out of His abundant love, God seeks to transform the world by providing justice for all His people.

Remember, to love God back, we must love the things He loves—and God loves justice. The prophet Isaiah, speaking the Word of God, said, "For I, the Lord, love justice; I hate robbery and iniquity" (Isa. 61:8). Interestingly, in Scripture God's love almost always refers directly to His people, but here we see that God has a passionate concern, a love, for the working of justice.

As leaders God calls us to love justice, to seek out injustice and confront it at every turn. "But you must return to your God; maintain love and justice, and wait for your God always" (Hos. 12:6). Love and justice are often combined in the Old Testament, but Jesus emphasized this almost synonymous relationship when He chastised the falsely pietistic. "But you neglect justice and the love of God" (Luke 11:42).

The Great Commandment leader, understanding that justice and love are inseparable, is always looking for ways he or she can alleviate injustice. The paradigm shift as it applies to justice is a movement away from reacting to injustice (or not being involved in rectifying injustices) to actively seeking out ways to confront injustice in the leader's milieu. Great Commandment leaders do so out of their love for God and their neighbors. They become Jesus's hands and feet to confront injustice anywhere so justice can flow like a river everywhere.

JUSTICE LIKE A RIVER

Because I'm a minister, those who don't believe in an all-powerful God often challenge me because they perceive so much injustice in the world. The most common question I hear is, "Where is God when horrible things happen to innocent people?" I understand that many who ask tough questions are sincerely searching for God in the midst of overwhelming tragedy. But on one occasion, while serving in Iraq, I discussed the issue of injustice several times with a friend and fellow officer. After we talked, I lovingly challenged him. "What are *you* doing to deal with evil and injustice in the world? Why do you continue to ask, 'Where is God?' Maybe God is asking why you sit back and enjoy a safe, prosperous life while so many others do not?"

My answer startled my friend, but it didn't satiate his appetite for divine intervention. He continued to be dogged by the idea that God, if He was all powerful, should miraculously intervene at every turn of injustice. My friend didn't stop asking, "Why is there is so much injustice in the world?"

Frankly, the Bible may not comprehensively address the origin or cause of evil and injustice. Many philosophers and theologians have debated the issue for millennia, and N. T. Wright also notes in his insightful book, *Evil and the Justice of God*, a lack of biblical clarity on the origin of evil. But Bishop Wright doesn't mince words in regard to the solution to injustice. God ultimately plans to end injustice, and that plan is His Son, Jesus Christ.[12] "A bruised reed he will not break, and a smoldering wick he will not snuff out. In faithfulness he will bring forth justice; he will not falter or be discouraged till he establishes justice on earth" (Isa. 42:3–4).

By coming to earth, God initiated His kingdom rule to finally and totally deal with evil and injustice in the world. After Jesus finished His work on earth and ascended into heaven,

He put His people in the lead to work for kingdom justice on earth. "Your kingdom come, your will be done on earth as it is in heaven" (Matt. 6:10).

The fact is, those in Christ are called to be on the injustice patrol. Jesus said, "Blessed are the peacemakers" (Matt. 5:9). We seek out injustices so we can be part of God's plan to create a just society that brings glory to Him.

In the end Jesus will correct every wrong and bring final justice to the world. But until then God intends that His chosen leaders bring justice to the oppressed, freedom to those in bondage, and recovery of sight to those blinded by evildoers. The prophet Amos expected that one day soon "justice [would] roll on like a river, righteousness like a never-failing stream!" (Amos 5:24).

JUSTICE FOR INDIVIDUALS

The call of God is clear. "What does the Lord require of you? To act justly and to love mercy and to walk humbly with your God" (Mic. 6:8). One of our primary functions as Great Commandment leaders is to act on behalf of those who've been denied what justly belongs to them, working for justice as part of the transformation process.

In the parable of the widow and the unjust judge (Luke 18:1–8), Jesus teaches His disciples how to pray with perseverance and to expect God to bring His justice to bear on unjust situations. In the parable Jesus tells the story of an ongoing dispute between a widow and a merciless judge, who finally relents because of her perseverance. Though Jesus doesn't compare God to an insensitive judge, He does make the correlation that persistence in praying to and trusting God results in His coming to our aid. "And will not God bring about justice for his chosen ones, who cry out to him day and night? Will he keep putting them off? I tell you, he will see that they get justice, and quickly" (Luke 18:7–8).

The first action of the Great Commandment leader is to pray on behalf of the oppressed. As we pray and listen to God, He will direct our paths to be involved in the ministry of justice to the oppressed. Prayer will help us discern where we should be involved.

pray for oppressed

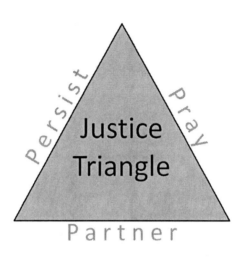

Two more actions are required if we plan to effectively engage in a ministry of justice. The second is partnership. We should be aware that God cares for all people. He is aware of the injustices being committed against His people (Ex. 3:7). As leaders seeking justice, we cannot assume we are the saviors of the people. Jesus is the Savior, and He is actively working on the issue He has brought to our attention. In addition, as we partner with God, He opens our eyes and prompts us to partner with other concerned people, agencies, and even the government. Some of the great justice victories in history were a combination of various groups, churches, non-profits, and government agencies working together in harmony to achieve a common goal.

partnering

Third, like the widow in the parable, we must learn to persist to see the issue through to the end. Those oppressed are

persist

unfortunately accustomed to others giving up on them. They have been burned by the evil systems perpetuating injustice. When we engage in justice ministries, it is imperative that we stay the course, no matter how difficult the trials become. God has shown us that through perseverance we will grow in His graces and achieve His perfect will (2 Peter 1:5–7; James 1:4; Heb. 10:36). ✓

STANDING WITH THE OPPRESSED

The oppressed often lack courage and are underequipped to deal with their circumstances. Those of us whom God has given wisdom, courage, power, and influence must use these gifts on behalf of those who do not have them. Remember, we should share every good gift we receive from God with His people. The ministry of mercy, goodness, and justice flow from God through His chosen leaders to the oppressed.

Finding the oppressed isn't difficult. Isaiah says we should "seek justice, encourage the oppressed. Defend the cause of the fatherless, plead the case of the widow" (Isa. 1:17). The apostle James also says, "Religion that God our Father accepts as pure and faultless is this: to look after orphans and widows in their distress and to keep oneself from being polluted by the world" (James 1:27). God, who desires justice, doesn't leave us without direction. Certainly those needing our special care and assistance include the wrongly imprisoned; those whom others have discriminated against because of race, color, gender, or ethnicity; and the physically and mentally challenged. The oppressed are all around us in every neighborhood and every society.

Nevertheless, we should ask God to give us wisdom to discern between those who are truly oppressed and those who erroneously perceive they are oppressed. An intrinsic connection exists not only between love and justice but also between truth and justice. "The works of his hands are faithful and just" (Ps. 111:7). The apostle Paul warned those who were poor due to their own laziness. "If a man will not work, he shall not eat" (2 Thess. 3:10). And for widows who had family members he had this advice: "But if a widow has children or grandchildren, these should learn first of all to put their religion into practice by caring for their own family and so repaying their parents and grandparents, for this is pleasing to God" (1 Tim. 5:4). In addition, Leviticus tells us that justice should not be perverted by showing "partiality to the poor or favoritism to the great" (Lev. 19:15). The motivation of our ministry of justice to the individual will come from both our deep love for God's people and our understanding of the truth of God's will for when, where, and with whom we should be involved.

ORGANIZATIONAL JUSTICE

One place where injustice seems to flourish is in organizations. Workers often feel they aren't dealt with fairly in regard to compensation, opportunities, or promotions in the workplace. Unions were established specifically to fight for workers' rights. For years the fact that women don't make the same salaries as their similarly qualified male counterparts has been well documented. People of color have often experienced discrimination when seeking jobs or getting promotions. Antidiscrimination laws have been enacted, equal opportunity commissions have been established, and quota systems have been put in place to deal with what appears to be institutionalized organizational injustice. Yet the problem of organizational injustice continues to plague most institutions and businesses.

Great Commandment leaders who lead churches, nonprofits, or for-profit organizations will be always confronted with the issue of injustice in the workplace because of humanity's sinful condition. The prophet Jeremiah warned businessmen, "Woe to him who builds his palace by unrighteousness, his upper rooms by injustice, making his countrymen work for nothing, not paying them for their labor" (Jer. 22:13). The writer of Proverbs said it would be better to gain "a little with righteousness than much gain with injustice" (Prov. 16:8). Even in the early church injustices against non-Jewish believers (Acts 6:1–7) required creating a system to deal with the problem. Developing systems of equity in institutions is difficult but important work.

Though God has been concerned with institutional injustice since ancient times, a secular theory of equity in the workplace didn't appear until John Stacey Adams put forth his vision in 1963. The website businessdictionary.com defines Adams's "equity theory" as the "concept that people derive job satisfaction and motivation by comparing their efforts (inputs) and income (outputs) with those of the other people in the same or other firms." If we feel we are working harder or better than our contemporaries, we should be promoted before them or given larger raises or bonuses. If those we perceive as not being as productive as we are get promoted or receive larger salary increases or bonuses, then, the theory states, our motivation will decrease. This theory has been tested, and research has generally supported the theory.[13]

We should be careful, however, about how we apply this theory. As Christians our primary motivation to work is not equity with others but Christ's love (2 Cor. 5:14) and honoring Him in all we do (Col. 3:23). The parable of the workers in the vineyard (Matt. 20:1–16) helps us understand that God wants to provide for all His people and that we shouldn't be jealous of what others have received. Instead, we should be grateful for what God has given us.

In the parable a vineyard owner hired several sets of workers at different times throughout the day. At the end of the day, each worker received the same amount of pay. Workers who had worked the longest hours complained about the seeming injustice, but the owner of the vineyard, who represents God in the parable, said, "Friend, I am not being unfair to you. Didn't you agree to work for a denarius? Take your pay and go. I want to give the man who was hired last the same as I gave you. Don't I have the right to do what I want with my own money? Or are you envious because I am generous?" (Matt. 20:13–15). *envy!* Sometimes we perceive injustice because of jealousy or envy. Though I've heard some say that someone's perception of truth is truth to him or her, only the truth is really true, not just the perception of it.

When I bought a home in 2008, I received a significant tax *Ex.-* credit I needed to pay back over fifteen years. I was extremely grateful for the influx of cash, but in 2009 the government offered the same tax credit without the need to repay it. My first thought was, *That's not fair!* After the Spirit jogged my memory about the above parable, however, I remembered God's incredible mercy and grace to me.

Interestingly, many of our soldiers serving in Iraq received the opportunity to take leave without charge because of a new program that started on a specific date in the middle of our deployment. Those who had already taken their leave before the date, however, didn't receive the same benefit. Though I didn't benefit from the program, I gave a briefing about the policy change. I told the soldiers that we needed to be grateful for what we had and not to be jealous of those who received the benefit (1 Thess. 5:18). The policy change was hard on some of them; they thought they should have received the same benefit other soldiers enjoyed. After the briefing some soldiers said, "These kinds of things happen all the time, Chaplain. In the end it all balances out." How true! In the end Jesus will right every wrong.

Jealousy and envy are sins. While diligently working for equity in our organizations, we Great Commandment leaders need to instruct Christians to understand that we ultimately labor for God, not men (Col. 3:23). Our rewards are being stored up for us in heaven.

COMMUNITY JUSTICE

Opportunities to work for justice for individuals and those in organizations are plentiful, but we need to be more proactive in seeking ways to work for justice in our communities. In one of the strangest stories in the Bible, God gave instructions to community leaders who'd come upon a murdered John Doe (Deut. 21:1–9). He told the priests from surrounding communities to measure the distance from their towns to the body. The community closest to the slain stranger would take responsibility for him. Though the story has many different applications, we learn that God is clearly concerned about each human life. The story also teaches that communities must take responsibility for what happens in their locale. God calls all community members, especially those who lead, to work for transformative justice in their community.

While serving as a church developer in the Bronx, I had the privilege to join a local community board. Several justice issues confronted our neighborhood. The city wanted to put a water-filtration plant in a local park. Several local landlords were warehousing their apartments. The area public hospital was going to close in favor of the larger, private hospital, which offered fewer amenities to the poor in our community. These issues required local citizens to speak up. Due to the large immigrant and poor population, however, they lacked a strong voice. The community board organized community members to work with the community power brokers and ensure that all of the community's concerns were heard. Even in a big city like New York, a significant need exists for people to be involved in the justice issues of each neighborhood.

Local churches can be involved in other community justice issues, including the following: working with the parks department to spruce up a local playground, taking part in a neighborhood watch, assisting with the hungry and homeless,

[handwritten margin notes: "take responsibility for your community"; "Examples of church involvement"]

or working to ensure that every community member has the opportunity to register to vote.

The church, a venerable member of each local community, has been given public benefits such as tax-free property, a source of income from the population, and other reduced costs due to its nonprofit nature. Since the community has given the church so many benefits, the church has the solemn responsibility to *give back to...* show its gratitude to the community by working for members who've been left out, left behind, or left alone through sin and injustice.

In the next and final chapter, we examine the "glocal" paradigm. This paradigm shift emphasizes that Christian leaders are also Great Commission leaders (Matt. 28:18–20). They aren't just concerned about their little slice of earth. God has called them to think globally because God is concerned about all the nations of the world. "Listen to me, my people…The law will go out from me; my justice will become a light to the nations" (Isa. 51:4). When Jesus was transfigured before Peter, James, and John, God said, "Here is my servant whom I have chosen, the one I love, in whom I delight; I will put my Spirit on him, and he will proclaim justice to the nations" (Matt. 12:18). We have been called to bring the message of God's love, salvation, and justice to a lost world. Therefore, we should be Christ's emissaries and provide justice to the oppressed. "As the Father has sent me, I am sending you" (John 20:21).

Chapter Review Questions   *? pg 162 bottom*

1. According to the author, "an intrinsic connection exists not only between love and justice but also between truth and justice." What does this statement mean to you?

2. Why is justice-seeking such an integral part of Great Commandment leadership?   *Part of what God calls believers to do*

look for "justice"

3. How might a Great Commandment leader personally and
    spiritually prepare to develop a just consciousness?
    pray it is exposed

4. What are some actions a Christian leader might engage in
    to bring about justice?   *Pg 160 "our focus"*

5. How might a Great Commandment leader engage the local
    church community in community justice issues?   *Pg 166 (bottom)*

Chapter 13

"Glocal" Paradigm

THE GREAT COMMISSION LEADER

GREAT COMMANDMENT LEADERS, who love the things God loves, are interested in seeing the whole world transformed for Christ (John 3:16; 2 Peter 3:9). Therefore, God has also called them to be Great Commission leaders. They read in Scripture of God's love for the whole world and are motivated to "go and make disciples of all nations" (Matt. 28:19).

The renowned missionary leader A. B. Simpson understood God's desire for the world to come to know Him. He resigned from his comfortable, upper-class church in Manhattan to minister to the poor immigrants in New York City and start a global missionary movement, the Christian and Missionary Alliance. Though Dr. Simpson never went overseas as a missionary, he ministered to the world in his backyard and founded one of the most effective missionary agencies in all of history. A. B. Simpson understood the "glocal" paradigm: serve globally by acting locally. He equipped thousands of missionaries to take the gospel to the whole world.

Before Jesus ascended to heaven, He commissioned His disciples to continue His global work. "But you will receive power when the Holy Spirit comes on you; and you will be my witnesses in Jerusalem, and in all Judea and Samaria, and to the ends of the earth" (Acts 1:8). Curiously, the King James Version uses the word *both* as the conjunction connecting all four of these distinct places. We have a sense here that Jesus is telling us that the church should be involved in missions in all four places at the same time. We don't first witness locally, then work our way out concentrically. No, we are supernaturally empowered to be involved in our locality, our region, and the far reaches of the planet.

Christ's global call to evangelize is not a new call; it's a correction to God's people in all generations who tend toward inward thinking and the localization of the gospel. Throughout history God called His people to go to the nations. "Sing to the Lord, all the earth; proclaim his salvation day after day. Declare his glory among the nations, his marvelous deeds among all peoples" (1 Chron. 16:23–24). Isaiah prophesied that God would make His people a "light for the Gentiles, that you may bring my salvation to the ends of the earth." (Isa. 49:6). Habakkuk saw a future where the whole "earth will be filled with the knowledge of the glory of the Lord, as the waters cover the sea" (Hab. 2:14). Jesus proclaimed with utter finality that the gospel "will be preached in the whole world as a testimony to all nations, and then the end will come" (Matt. 24:14).

THE "GLOCAL" MISSIONS PARADIGM

How can we accomplish this work in all of these places at the same time? Each of us empirically experiences the world from a local place; our senses are confined to the place we are in. In church history a specialized division of labor (missionaries, pastors, evangelists, and so on) was needed to accomplish the global mission of the church. But today the world has been brought to every individual by the forces of globalization through immigration, technology, and mass media. We are, as Joshua Meyrowitz said, "inside and outside at the same time. We now live in 'glocalities.' Each glocality is unique in many ways, and yet each is also influenced by global trends and global consciousness."[14] The world has come into our living rooms and neighborhoods.

we have global contact

Thomas Friedman's book *The World Is Flat* is a wonderful foray into how much the world has come into our local lives. In the book Friedman takes us on a whirlwind tour around the world, but we feel like we've never left our homes. Surprisingly, we might find that when we dial a local number to order a pizza, we might actually be talking to someone in India. With outsourcing, the Internet, expatriate global workers, work-flow software, blogging, and podcasting, people are acting locally and serving globally.

As we serve globally in our localities, we begin to see that we can influence the world for Christ, sometimes without leaving our own homes. The Internet and wireless technology have changed the way we communicate in ways we still cannot fully understand. What is clear is that we're now able to touch people across the world from our offices, dorms, and living rooms. Many local church pastors podcast their sermons on the World Wide Web, and some have been surprised to discover that hundreds or thousands around the world are tuning in.

But it isn't technology alone that has flattened our world. While pastoring a local church in a suburb of Pittsburgh, I began to see the possibilities of "glocalism" by reaching our local community for Christ. Unlike A. B. Simpson, who had trouble convincing his parishioners of the need to send cross-cultural missionaries to far-off countries, our challenge is to convince our traditionally "missionary-minded" congregants that the world has come to our neighborhood; so we also need to send cross-cultural missionaries to those living in our own backyards.

My mother-in-law has always been a staunch supporter of overseas missionaries, but until she saw the cross-cultural work we were doing in our own neighborhood, she didn't think of it as missionary work. Now that she's participated in the work, she's a true believer in the "glocal" paradigm of missions. Many are still stuck in the old paradigm and believe that the only way to do missions is to spend a lifetime among 'the heathen in the dark areas of the far-off world.' But when you open your eyes and mind to serve globally in your own backyard, you'll begin to see the endless possibilities of touching the world for Christ.

One key difference between "glocal" missions and traditional missions is that within a local ministry, everyone is involved, not just a select few. The essence of "glocality" is communal. It requires all members of a local ministry to participate. How will this look?

"INTRAFUGE"

In Old Testament times, God called the Israelites to be a light to the nations (Isa. 42:6), but generally the Jewish people exerted little movement to evangelize in distant lands. Even the Diaspora tended to be inward focused since the Jewish people didn't want to be contaminated by the pagans surrounding them. Yet God still longed for the Israelites to transform the world. He even sent one of His prophets against his will to save an entire nation (Jonah 1). Though ancient Israelites didn't obey God's command to be a light to the Gentiles, the Word of God still transformed many non-Jews. Ancient Jerusalem became an important city for worldwide trade; therefore, many people were drawn to God in Israel by a force they couldn't understand.

One could say that during Old Testament times centripetal force drew people to God in Israel. Isaac Newton first described this force as one by "which bodies are drawn or impelled, or in any way tend, towards a point as to a center." Because an entire nation believed God was worshipped 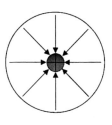 in a particular place, their lives and economy revolved around the temple. Therefore, any foreigners involved with the Israelites were drawn to their spiritual center. Similarly, the transformative gospel, when preached faithfully in any area, will have the same effect. The gospel will draw people in. "But I, when I am lifted up from the earth, will draw all men to myself" (John 12:32). If we do not equip and send forth disciples, however, the work will remain localized.

After Jesus commissioned the disciples, He sent them into the world. There was no confusion about the call. The disciples were being sent; like soldiers they were to travel and to ensure that the gospel was taken to the uttermost ends of the earth. "He said 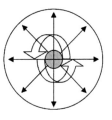 to them, 'Go into all the world and preach the good news to all creation'" (Mark 16:15). The Holy Spirit was the power behind the mission (Acts 1:8), and an almost centrifugal force pushed the Word to every people group around the world. This amazing "force" spread the gospel around the world with amazing speed and eternal effect.

In the twenty-first century, due to the advent of globalization, the Great Commandment leader will use a new kind of force. It could be called "intrafuge" or an "intrafugal force," a force characterized 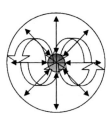 by a paradoxical combination of both centrifugal and centripetal forces working simultaneously. The effect is that individuals will be not only drawn to the gospel in a local area but also compelled to spread the gospel to the ends of the earth. When we understand that God's hand is "flattening the earth" for the purpose of spreading the gospel worldwide, the Great Commandment leader will lead transformational missions locally, regionally, and globally.

FOUR "GLOCAL" WAYS TO TRANSFORM THE WORLD

Without minimizing the critical need for Great Commandment leaders to raise up, train, and send forth traditional cross-cultural missionaries around the globe, especially to unreached people groups, I offer four ways we can "glocally" transform the world for Christ.

First, when Jesus commissioned us to work in our local communities, in surrounding communities, in our regions, and in distant places around the globe, He gave us a transcultural model for missions (Acts 1:8). At Crestmont Alliance Church we trained church members to evangelize their neighbors (Jerusalem), developed ministries of outreach and justice in our nearest and poorest community (Judea), sent teams to West Virginia each year to work in a specific hurting community (Samaria), and sent a team on an annual trip to assist a missionary couple in Mexico (international).

Though much of what we did was short-term ministry, the church is committed to these ministries for the long term. Relationships have been established, and trust has been built; therefore, each year the ministry's effectiveness grows. It should be noted that we do not need to have a large ministry to accomplish the Acts 1:8, four-fold mission's strategy. Crestmont Alliance Church had only about 225 members when we implemented our Acts 1:8 model.

As a Great Commandment leader who is faithful to the Great Commission, you should be able to point to how you and your ministry are personally fulfilling the Acts 1:8 commission. I can't think of a better way to equip Christians to be involved in cross-cultural ministry than to get them to participate in a short-term mission experience (see "pedagogical method" in Chapter 8).

Second, because of the new influx of foreign nationals to the United States, plenty of opportunities exist to work with internationals in just about every community. In Queens, New York, one of the most diverse places in the United States, one would be hard-pressed not to work with people from different countries. Though cross-cultural work is long and slow, planted seeds can produce great fruit long after we're gone. If you don't live in a metropolitan area, your local college or university undoubtedly offers people from different ethnic and racial groups.

For years, Campus Crusade and InterVarsity have conducted successful ministries to international students. One benefit of working with international students who are living in the United States on student visas is that many return to their home countries. If you can successfully disciple just one person from another country, you might start a movement of Christianity where that student and his or her family live. In Acts 8, a miraculous story of transformation takes place between Philip and an Ethiopian government official. There in the Israeli desert, an unnamed Ethiopian received Christ and was baptized after coming to understand the Scriptures about Jesus. It's possible that this same Ethiopian started the Ethiopian Coptic Church, one of the oldest Christian churches in the world. Touch just one international student in your locality, and you may change the world for Christ forever.

Third is the ministry of "cross-cultural tentmaking." The apostle Paul worked in the construction of tents to support his ministry. Regardless of where he went, if he needed to make money, he was able to earn his keep (Acts 18:13). Paul traveled the world and spread the gospel while making good contacts in his trade. Over the last century many missions agencies have recruited modern-day "tentmakers," professionals sent to other countries to employ their professional skills and work as missionaries.

Just a few years ago, because of the rise of the service industry, it was said that if you wanted to get a good job, you needed to be willing to move to another city or state. Today, more employers are asking potential workers to be willing to work not only in another state but also in other countries. God is calling a new generation of "tentmakers" to respond to this new "flat earth."

Today more than four million expatriate American workers live around the world, and the number is increasing each year. Forty million expatriates from other countries live in the United States. Within the Christian and Missionary Alliance (C&MA) denomination is an agency called the International Fellowship of Alliance Professionals (IFAP), an association of expatriates working in foreign countries, many of whom do not allow traditional missionaries, and spreading the good news to those who may have never heard it before.

Finally, the World Wide Web is another effective way to touch the world for Christ. Through podcasting, blogging, and virtual churches, millions, maybe even billions, are exposed to the transformational message of Jesus Christ. Most of us don't even need to leave our homes or offices to reach people around the world. We can truly minister locally and serve globally.

Though some believe the web is getting overcrowded with Christian sites, the more American Christians participate in intentionally trying to reach a foreign audience the better.

The work of transforming God's people is an ongoing, worldwide enterprise. Great Commandment leaders see beyond the horizon of their locality and envision how they and their followers can become globally engaged. They personify the message of John 3:16 for themselves and every one they lead. "For God so loved the world that he gave his one and only Son, that whoever believes in him shall not perish but have eternal life." Jesus tells us to go and make disciples, and we can now go "glocal" and fulfill that mandate.

Chapter Review Questions

1. What Great Commandment lessons might we learn from A. B. Simpson?
2. What is "glocal?"
3. How might you raise global awareness in your local context?
4. Describe four "glocal" ways to transform the world.
5. Why is developing a "glocal" worldview essential for Great Commandment leaders?

Postlude: Urbi et Orbi

AFTER MUCH PRAYER Josh decided to send an e-mail describing the inequity in the admissions process to the vice president of hospital affairs. The vice president then forwarded the e-mail to the hospital president. Much to Josh's surprise, though his supervisor wasn't happy with him, the president e-mailed Josh back and thanked him for bringing the matter to his attention. The president was grateful that the information was kept in house, and he decided to make the matter public to display the hospital's transparent management style.

At the press conference, where the problem was exposed, Josh was introduced as the employee who discovered the problem and who, with the hospital's full support, was now in charge of finding the solution to eliminate discrimination in the admissions process. About a year later, Josh and the hospital received an award from the NAACP for their work for racial justice.

Soon after the press conference, Josh's life changed radically when he met Maritza, a woman from Honduras, at his church. The two had a similar love for those who were hurting. Maritza worked as a home health aide and had a deep passion for caring for the sick.

They dated for several months and ministered together to young people from the community and to those who worked at the hospital. Soon they were engaged, and a year later they were married in Tegucigalpa, the city where Maritza was born. By the time Josh married Maritza, he'd learned to speak Spanish fluently and was interested in Latin American culture.

One Christmas Day, Josh and Maritza watched Pope Benedict on television give his blessing to the people at St. Peter's Basilica. The announcer noted that the blessing was known as the *Urbi et Orbi*. Translated from the Latin, it was a blessing "to the city, to the world." When he heard the phrase, Josh felt a nudge from the Spirit that he should be a blessing not only to the people of his city but also to the world. Josh and Maritza prayed and asked God to guide them to where and how He wanted them to make disciples of the nations.

Josh's Bible study at the hospital continued to grow and attracted several doctors, who were members of the Christian Physicians Association. All of the doctors were part of churches in the wealthy suburbs where they lived. Sadly, none of the doctors were involved in ministry in their local churches because they were always too busy at work. Josh talked to them about making an impact in the local community. One of the doctors said, "I really sense that God is calling me to do something for the poor outside the United States." Therefore, the group prayed about the potential of doing overseas ministry.

Maritza, part of the lunch Bible study, spoke about the poor in Honduras and about how most in her village lacked medical care. After much prayer and consultation with a pastor from Maritza's village, the members of the Bible study decided to adopt the church and the community. The Bible study group, a team of seven doctors from the hospital, along with Josh and Maritza, went on an initial visit to Honduras. While they were there, they saw the poverty of the people and decided to set a goal to build a health clinic in the village outside Tegucigalpa. Each doctor used two weeks of his vacation to go to Honduras, take care of the sick, and proclaim the gospel.

Doctors from the initial team recruited other doctors, who also went and served on a two-week rotation. Soon they had enough doctors to staff the clinic year-round. They trained local members of the village to serve as assistants to the doctors.

Josh and Maritza continued to work with youth in the neighborhood and support new church planters from their church. Each year they took a trip to Honduras to pray, care for the sick, and share the gospel with the locals. The church in Honduras grew, and life significantly improved in that little village.

One year Josh spoke to the church in Honduras and inspired the congregation with a sermon that echoed the speech of the pastor who'd spoken at his graduation years before. After he challenged the church to love God back, he gave them five words to guide them in living a God-honoring life.

"With these five little words, you'll live a life that will change the world forever for Christ," he said. "Are you ready for the five words? Here they are: do great things for God!" After the translation, Josh asked, "What are you going to do?"

The church responded in unison, "Do great things for God!"

The Greek word for "greatest" in the Great Commandment is *megas*. Today we use that word to describe many eternally un-important things: megamillions (lottery), megastars, megamalls, megamodels, even a rock band call Megadeth. But as we are called to be leaders in God's kingdom, we are filled and motivated by

God's megalove for us. We respond with megagratitude, and we envision and fulfill megadreams to expand His kingdom rule. The Great Commandment reminds us that we can do great things for our great God because of His great love, power, and presence in our lives. Go and do great things for God!

Endnotes

1. "Deification," *The Orthodox Study Bible* (Nashville: Thomas Nelson, 2008), 1692.
2. Bede, "Exposition on the Gospel of Mark 2:22," *Cetedoc Library of Christian Latin Texts*: CLCLT-4 on CD-ROM, ed. P. Tombeaur (Turnhout: Brepols, 2000), quoted in Thomas C. Oden and Christopher A. Hall, eds., *Ancient Christian Commentary on Scripture* (Downers Grove, IL: InterVarsity Press, 1998), 165.
3. Origen, "Commentary on Matthew 2," *Die Griechischen Christlichen Schriftsteller* (Berlin: Akademie-Verlag, 1897), quoted in Thomas C. Oden and Christopher A. Hall, eds., *Ancient Christian Commentary on Scripture* (Downers Grove, IL: InterVarsity Press, 1998), 157.
4. The idea for this commencement address was adapted from an address given at Nyack College by Rev. Pete Schwalm, pastor emeritus of Fairhaven Church, Dayton, Ohio.
5. Henry Blackaby and Richard Blackaby with Claude King, *Seven Truths from Experiencing God* (Nashville: Lifeway Press, 2007), 18.

6. John MacArthur, *The Gospel According to Jesus* (Grand Rapids: Zondervan, 2008), 30.
7. Jim Collins, *Good to Great* (New York: HarperCollins), 39-40.
8. Bernard M. Bass, *Bass & Stogdill's Handbook of Leadership* (New York: Free Press, 1990), 218.
9. Peter G. Northouse, *Leadership: Theory and Practice* (London: Sage Publications, 2009), 170-178.
10. George Barna, "Barna Survey Examines Changes in Worldview Among Christian over the Past 13 Years," March 6, 2009. Online article downloaded on October 1, 2010 from http://www.barna.org/barna-update/article/21-transformation/252-barna-survey-examines-changes-in-worldview-among-christians-over-the-past-13-years?q=less+percent+christians+have+biblical+worldview
11. Tom Etema, *Events Are Never Enough*, Unpublished E-Book, downloaded October 1, 2010 from http://www.iequip.org/atf/cf/%7BB11550F8-928E-4495-A24A-C10C76662C86%7D/EVENTS.PDF.
12. N.T. Wright, *Evil and the Justice of God* (Downers Grove, IL: InterVartsity Press, 2006), Chapter 1.
13. Paul S. Goodman and Abraham Friedman, "An Examination of Adams Theory of Equity," *Administrative Science Quarterly* 16, no. 3 (September 1971): 271–278.
14. Joshua Meyrowitz, "The Rise of Glocality: New Senses of Place and Identity in the Global Village," (2004): 23. Unpublished E-Essay downloaded October 1, 2010 from http://www.socialscience.t-mobile.hu/dok/8_Meyrowitz.pdf.

Breinigsville, PA USA
02 March 2011
256814BV00001B/2/P